CONSOLATIONS

Also by David Whyte

POETRY

Songs for Coming Home

Where Many Rivers Meet

Fire in the Earth

The House of Belonging

Everything Is Waiting for You

River Flow: New and Selected Poems

Pilgrim

The Bell and the Blackbird

David Whyte: Essentials

PROSE

The Heart Aroused: Poetry and the Preservation of the Soul in Corporate America

Crossing the Unknown Sea: Work as a Pilgrimage of Identity

The Three Marrriages: Reimagining Work, Self and Relationship

CONSOLATIONS

The SOLACE,

NOURISHMENT *and*

UNDERLYING MEANING

of EVERYDAY WORDS

DAVID WHYTE

Introduced by Maria Popova

CANONGATE

First published in Great Britain in 2019 by Canongate Books Ltd,
14 High Street, Edinburgh EH1 1TE

canongate.co.uk

8

First published in the USA in 2015 by
Many Rivers Press, P.O. Box 868, Langley WA 98260, USA

British Library Cataloguing-in-Publication Data
A catalogue record for this book is available on
request from the British Library

ISBN 978 1 78689 763 3

Typeset in Bembo by
Palimpsest Book Production Ltd, Falkirk, Stirlingshire

Printed and bound in Great Britain by
Clays Ltd, Elcograf S.p.A.

MIX
Paper from
responsible sources
FSC
www.fsc.org   FSC® C018072

Dedicated to
WORDS
and their
beautiful, hidden and beckoning
uncertainties

The Publisher would like to express his deep gratitude and love for Silvie, without whom this edition of *Consolations* would not exist. Thank you for sending me Honesty, the first piece I read in this book, and for introducing me to Maria Popova's work.

And On Being. Your Fingerprints are Everywhere.

CONTENTS

INTRODUCTION

'Words belong to each other,' Virginia Woolf's scratchy voice unspools from the only surviving recording of her aural presence. Indeed, words are our creation, but our Pygmalian love for them must not deceive us – they do not belong to us, for they are not static figures of thought to be owned and traded as artefacts. They are living organisms, elastic and porous, feral with meaning, ever-evolving. They possess us more than we possess them. They feed on us more than we feed on them. Words belong to each other, and we to them.

And yet the commonest words in our lexicon – those tasked with containing and conveying the most elemental human truths and experiences – are slowly being shorn of meaning: assaulted by misuse, abraded by overuse, overthought and underconsidered, trampled of dimension and discoloured of nuance.

In *Consolations*, David Whyte repatriates us in the

land of language by giving words back to themselves and, in this generous act, giving us back to ourselves – we, sensemaking creatures who navigate this old maze of a world through the mightiest figuring faculty we have: language itself. For each word he chooses – *anger, longing, silence* – Whyte composes less a redefinition than a reanimation, less Cawdrey than Montaigne. There is tremendous kindness and generosity of spirit under-girding his micro-essays, reinstating each word and the meaning it carries as a truth not only human but humane. 'Friendship is a mirror to presence and a testament to forgiveness,' he writes of a word so hollowed in our era of social media 'friends', in our culture so conditioned on unforgiving cynicism and distracted flight from presence. On the enchanted loom of his poetic imagination, Whyte mends these most threadbare words into splendid tapestries of thought and feeling, lush with reclaimed meaning. What emerges is that supreme gift of being: a deeper sense of belonging – of words, to words, and to ourselves.

Maria Popova

ALONE

is a word that stands by itself, carrying the austere, solitary beauty of its own meaning even as it is spoken to another. It is a word that can be felt at the same time as an invitation to depth and as an imminent threat, as in 'all alone', with its returned echo of abandonment. 'Alone' is a word that rings with a strange finality, especially when contained in that haunting aggregate, 'left all alone', as if the state once experienced begins to define and engender its own inescapable world. The first step in spending time alone is to admit how afraid of it we are.

Being alone is a difficult discipline: a beautiful and difficult sense of being solitary is always the ground from which we step into a contemplative intimacy with the unknown, but the first portal of aloneness is often experienced as a gateway to alienation, grief and abandonment. To find ourselves alone or to be left alone is an ever-present, fearful and abiding human potentiality of which we are often unconsciously, and deeply, afraid.

To be alone for any length of time is to shed an outer skin. The body is inhabited in a different way when we are alone than when we are with others. Alone, we live in our bodies as a question rather than a statement.

The permeability of being alone asks us to re-imagine ourselves, to become impatient with ourselves, to tire of the same old story and then slowly, hour by hour, to start to tell the story in a different way, as other parallel ears, ones we were previously unaware of, begin to listen to us more carefully in the silence. For a solitary life to flourish, even if it is only for a few precious hours, aloneness asks us to make a friend of silence, and just as importantly to inhabit that silence in our own particular way, to find our very own way into our own particular, and even virtuoso, way of being alone.

To inhabit silence in our aloneness is to stop telling

the story altogether. To begin with, aloneness always leads to rawness and vulnerability, to a fearful simplicity, to not recognising and to not knowing, to the wish to find any company other than that not knowing, unknown self, looking back at us in the silent mirror.

One of the elemental dynamics of self-compassion is to understand our deep reluctance to be left to ourselves.

Aloneness begins in puzzlement at our own reflection, transits through awkwardness and even ugliness at what we see, and culminates, one appointed hour or day, in a beautiful unlooked-for surprise, at the new complexion beginning to form, the slow knitting together of an inner life, now exposed to air and light.

To be alone is not necessarily to be absent from the company of others; the radical step is to let ourselves alone, to cease the berating voice that is constantly trying to interpret and force the story from too small and too complicated a perspective.

Even in company, a sense of imminent aloneness is a quality that can be cultivated. Aloneness does not need a desert, or a broad ocean, or a quiet mountain; human beings have the ability to feel the rawest, most intimate forms of aloneness whilst living closely with others or beset by the busyness of the world. They can feel alone around a meeting table, in the happiest, most committed marriage, or aboard a crowded ship with a full complement of crew.

The difficulty of being alone may be felt most keenly in the most intimate circumstances, in the darkness of the marriage bed: one centimetre and a thousand miles apart, or in the silence around a tiny crowded kitchen table. But to feel alone in the presence of others is also to understand the singularity of human existence whilst experiencing the deep physical current that binds us to others whether we want that binding or no: aloneness can measure togetherness even through a sense of distance.

At the beginning of the twenty-first century, to feel alone or want to be alone is deeply unfashionable: to admit to feeling alone is to reject and betray others, as if they are not good company, and do not have entertaining, interesting lives of their own to distract us; and to actually seek to be alone is a radical act. To want to be alone is to refuse a certain kind of conversational hospitality and to turn to another door, and another kind of welcome, not necessarily defined by human vocabulary.

It may be that time away from a work, an idea of ourselves, or a committed partner is the very essence of appreciation for the other, for the work and for the life of another; to be able to let them alone as we let ourselves alone, to live something that feels like a choice again, to find ourselves alone as a looked-for achievement, not a state to which we have been condemned.

AMBITION

is a word that lacks any real ambition. Ambition is desire frozen, the current of a vocational life immobilised and over-concretised to set, unforgiving goals. Ambition may be essential for the young and as yet unrealised life, but becomes the essential obstacle of any mature life. Ambition abstracts us from the underlying elemental nature of the creative conversation while providing us the cover of a target that has become false through over-description, overfamiliarity or too much understanding.

The ease of having an ambition is that it can be explained to others; the very disease of ambition is that it can be so easily explained to others. What is worthy of a life's dedication does not want to be known by us in ways that diminish its actual sense of presence. Everything true to itself has its own secret language and an internal intentionality with a secret, surprising flow, even to the person who supposedly puts it all in motion.

Ambition ultimately withers all secrets in its glare before those secrets have had time to come to life from within, and then thwarts the generosity and maturity that ripens the discourse of a lifetime's dedication to a work.

We may direct the beam of ambition to illuminate a certain corner of the future world, but ultimately it can reveal to us only those dreams with which we have already become familiar. Ambition left to itself, like the identity of the average billionaire, always becomes tedious, its only object the creation of larger and larger empires of control; but a true vocation calls us out beyond ourselves, breaks our heart in the process and then humbles, simplifies and enlightens us about the hidden, core nature of the work that enticed us in the first place. We find that, all along, we had what we needed from the beginning and that in the end we have returned to its essence, an essence we could not understand until we had experienced the actual heartbreak of the journey.

No matter the self-conceited importance of our labours we are all compost for worlds we cannot yet imagine. Ambition takes us toward that horizon, but not over it – that line will always recede before our controlling hands. But a calling is a conversation between our physical bodies, our work, our intellects and imaginations, and a new world that is itself the territory we seek. A vocation always includes the specific, heartrending way we will fail at our attempt to live fully. A true vocation always metamorphoses both ambition and failure into compassion and under-standing for others.

Ambition takes willpower and constant applications of energy to stay on a perceived bearing; but a serious vocational calling demands a constant attention to the unknown gravitational field that surrounds us and from which we recharge ourselves, as if breathing from the atmosphere of possibility itself. A life's work is not a series of stepping-stones, onto which we calmly place our feet, but more like an ocean crossing where there is no path, only a heading, a direction, in conversation with the elements. Looking back, we see the wake we have left as only a brief glimmering trace on the waters.

Ambition is natural to the first steps of youth, who must experience its essential falsity to know the larger reality that stands behind it, but held on to too long, and especially in eldership, it always comes to lack surprise, turns the last years of the ambitious into a second childhood, and makes the once successful into an object of pity.

The authentic watermark running through the background of a life's work is an arrival at generosity and, as a mark of that generosity, delight in the hopes of the young: and the giving away to them, not only of rewards that may have been earned but the reward in the secret itself, the core artistry that made the journey a journey.

Perhaps the greatest legacy we can leave from our work is not to instil ambition in others, though this may be the first way we describe its arrival in our life, but the passing on of a sense of sheer privilege, of having found a road, a way to follow, and then having been allowed to walk it, often with others, with all its difficulties and minor triumphs; the underlying primary gift of having been both a witness to and a full participant in the conversation.

ANGER

is the deepest form of care, for another, for the world, for the self, for a life, for the body, for a family and for all our ideals, all vulnerable and all, possibly, about to be hurt.

Stripped of physical imprisonment and violent reaction, anger points toward the purest form of compassion; the internal living flame of anger always illuminates what we belong to, what we wish to protect and those things for which we are willing to hazard and even imperil ourselves.

What we usually call anger is only what is left of its essence when we are overwhelmed by its accompanying vulnerability, when it reaches the lost surface of our mind or our body's incapacity to hold it, or when it touches the limits of our understanding. What we name as anger is actually only the incoherent physical incapacity to sustain this deep form of care in our outer daily life; the unwillingness to be large enough and generous enough to hold what we love helplessly in our bodies or our minds with the clarity and breadth of our whole being.

What we have named as anger on the surface is the violent outer response to our own inner powerlessness, a powerlessness connected to such a profound sense of rawness and care that it can find no proper outer body or identity or voice, or way of life to hold it.

What we call anger is often simply the unwillingness to live the full measure of our fears or of our not knowing, in the face of our love for a wife, in the depth of our caring for a son, in our wanting the best, in the face of simply being alive and loving those with whom we live.

Our anger breaks to the surface most often through our feeling there is something profoundly wrong with this powerlessness and vulnerability; anger too often finds its voice strangely, through our incoherence and through our inability to speak, but anger in its pure state is the measure of the way we are implicated in the world and made vulnerable through love in all its specifics: a daughter, a house, a family, an enterprise, a land or a colleague.

Anger turns to violence and violent speech when the mind refuses to countenance the vulnerability of the body in its love for all these outer things – we are often abused or have been abused by those who love us but have no vehicle to carry its understanding, or who have no outer emblems of their inner care or even their own wanting to be wanted. Lacking any outer vehicle for the expression of this inner rawness they are simply overwhelmed by the elemental nature of love's vulnerability. In their helplessness they turn their violence on the very people who are the outer representation of this inner lack of control.

But anger truly felt at its centre is the essential living flame of being fully alive and fully here; it is a quality to be followed to its source, to be prized, to be tended, and an invitation to finding a way to bring that source fully into the world through making the mind clearer and more generous, the heart more compassionate, and the body larger and strong enough to hold it.

What we call anger on the surface only serves to define its true underlying quality by being a complete but absolute mirror-opposite of its true internal essence.

BEAUTY

is the harvest of presence, the evanescent moment of
seeing or hearing on the outside what already lives far
inside us; the eyes, the ears or the imagination suddenly
become a bridge between the here and the there,
between then and now, between the inside and the
outside; beauty is the conversation between what we
think is happening outside in the world and what is
just about to occur far inside us.

Beauty is an achieved state of both deep attention
and self-forgetting: the self-forgetting of seeing, hearing,
smelling or touching that erases our separation, our
distance, our fear of the other. Beauty invites us, through
entrancement, to that fearful frontier between what
we think makes us; and what we think makes the
world. Beauty is almost always found in symmetries
and intriguing asymmetries: the symmetries and asymmetries seen out in creation, the wings of the moth,

the airy sky and the solid earth, the restful, focused eyes of a loving face in which we see our own self reflected: the symmetry also, therefore, of bringing together inner and outer recognitions, the far horizon of otherness seen in that face joined to the deep inner horizon of our own being. Beauty is an inner and an outer complexion living in one face.

Beauty especially occurs in the meeting of time with the timeless; the passing moment framed by what has happened and what is about to occur: the scattering of the first spring apple blossom, the turning, spiralling flight of a curled leaf in the falling light; the smoothing of white sun-filled sheets by careful hands setting them to air on a line, the broad expanse of cotton filled by the breeze only for a moment, the sheets sailing on into dryness, billowing toward a future that is always beckoning, always just beyond us. Beauty is the harvest of presence.

BEGINNING

well or beginning poorly, what is important is simply to begin, but the ability to make a good beginning is also an art form. Like picking up a new and unfamiliar musical instrument, the first necessary step involves taking the time to get a simple clear note, usually the simple clear note of forgiveness that comes in allowing yourself the right, at this stage, not to know anything at all. Beginning anything well involves a clearing away of the confusing, the cluttered and the complicated to find the beautiful, often hidden lineaments of the essential and the necessary.

Beginning is difficult, and our insulating rituals and the virtuoso subtleties of our methods of delay are always a fine, ever-present measure of our reluctance in taking that first close-in, courageous step to reclaiming the happiness of actually having started.

Perhaps, because taking a new step always begins

from the central, foundational core of the body, a body we have neglected, beginning well means seating ourselves in the body again, catching up with ourselves and the person we have become since we last tried to begin. This radical physical embodiment leads to an equally radical internal simplification, where, suddenly, very large parts of us, parts of us we have kept gainfully employed for years, parts of us still rehearsing the old complicated story, are suddenly out of a job.

There occurs, in effect, a form of internal corporate downsizing, where the parts of us too afraid to participate or having nothing now to offer, are let go, with all of the accompanying death-like trauma, and where the very last fight occurs, a rear-guard disbelief that this new, less complicated self, and this very simple step, is all that is needed for the new possibilities ahead.

It is always hard to believe that the courageous step is so close to us, that it is closer than we ever could imagine, that in fact we already know what it is, and that the step is simpler, more radical than we had thought: just picking up the pen or the wood chisel, just picking up the instrument or the phone, which is why we so often prefer the story to be more elaborate, our identities to be safely clouded by fear, why we want the horizon to remain always in the distance, the promise never fully and simply made, the essay longer than it needs to be and the answer safely in the realm of impossibility.

BESIEGED

is how most people feel most of the time: by events, by people, by all the necessities of providing, parenting or participating, by creative possibilities they have set in motion themselves; and strangely, most strongly besieged by a success they have achieved through long years of endeavour.

To feel crowded, set upon, blocked by circumstances, in defeat or victory, is not only the daily experience of most human beings in most contemporary societies, it has been an abiding dynamic of individual life since the dawn of human consciousness. In a human life there is no escape from commitment: retreat to a desert island and the lonely islander will draw up a Robinson Crusoe list to make the place habitable or begin building a raft to escape; tell everyone to go away and they hang around wanting to know why. Earn a great deal of money to gain individual freedom and a whole world moves in for a share of the harvest.

If the world will not go away, then the great discipline seems to be the ability to make an identity that can live in the midst of everything without feeling beset. Being besieged asks us to begin the day not with a *to do* list but a *not to do* list, a moment outside of the time-bound world in which it can be reordered and reprioritised. In this space of undoing and silence we create a foundation from which to re-imagine our day and ourselves. Beginning the daily conversation from a point of view of freedom and being untethered allows us to re-see ourselves, to re-enter the world as if for the first time. We give ourselves and our accomplishments, our ambitions and our over-described hopes away, in order to see in what form they return to us.

To lift the siege, we do our best for our children, but then, at the right time, send them off with a blessing, no matter their perilous direction. We run a business while remembering, as the overhead grows, how the enterprise was originally our doorway to freedom. We celebrate success but realise that another horizon now beckons, that we have in effect to start again, many times over. To get the measure of our success, we learn to call for an intimate close-in interiority, rather than a hoped-for, unattainable, far-and-away.

Besieged as we are, little wonder that men and women alternate between the dream of a place apart, untouched by the world, and then wanting to be wanted again in that aloneness. Besieged or left alone, we seem to live best at the crossroad between irretrievable aloneness and irretrievable belonging, and even better, as a conversation between the two where no choice is available. We are both: other people will never go away, and aloneness is both possible and necessary.

Creating a state of aloneness in the besieged everyday may be one of the bravest things individual men and women can do for themselves. *Nel mezzo*, in the midst of everything, as Dante said, to be besieged – but beautifully, because we have made a place to stand in the people and the places and the perplexities we have grown to love, seeing them not now as enemies or forces laying siege but, as if for the first time, as participants in the drama, both familiar and strangely surprising. We find that having people knock on our door is as much a privilege as it is a burden; that being seen, being recognised and being wanted by the world, and having a place in which to receive everyone and everything, is infinitely preferable to its opposite.

CLOSE

is what we almost always are: close to happiness, close to another, close to leaving, close to tears, close to God, close to losing faith, close to being done, close to saying something or close to success, and even, with the greatest sense of satisfaction, close to giving the whole thing up.

Our human essence lies not in arrival, but in being almost there: we are creatures who are on the way, our journey a series of impending anticipated arrivals. We live by unconsciously measuring the inverse distances of our proximity: an intimacy calibrated by the vulnerability we feel in giving up our sense of separation.

To go beyond our normal identities and become closer than close is to lose our sense of self in temporary joy, a form of arrival that only opens us to deeper forms of intimacy that blur our fixed, controlling, surface identities.

To consciously become close is a courageous form of unilateral disarmament, a chancing of our arm and our love, a willingness to hazard our affections and an unconscious declaration that we might be equal to the inevitable loss that the vulnerability of being close will bring.

Human beings do not find their essence through fulfilment or eventual arrival but by staying close to the way they like to travel, to the way they hold the conversation between the ground on which they stand and the horizon to which they go. We are, in effect, always close, always close to the ultimate secret: that we are more real in our simple wish to find a way than any destination we could reach; the step between not understanding that and understanding that is as close as we get to happiness.

CONFESSION

is a stripping away of protection, the telling of a truth which might once have seemed like a humiliation, become suddenly a gateway, an entrance to solid ground; even a first step home. To confess is to free oneself, not only by admitting a sin or an omission but to profess a deeper allegiance, a greater dedication to something beyond the mere threat of immediate punishment or the desolation of being shunned. To confess is to declare oneself ready for a more courageous road, one in which a previously defended identity might not only be shorn away but seen to be irrelevant – a distraction, a working delusion that kept us busy over the years and held us unaccountable to the real question.

Freedom from deception may be the goal, but no confession is without consequences. Our fears about the result of confessing are well grounded: the old identity the secret was protecting almost never survives the revelation. We begin the new life in isolation, perhaps indeed shunned by those we have wronged or even by those unable to understand our need to tell. Confession implicitly calls for carrying on the journey newly alone, unaccompanied by the familiar company we have kept until now.

Deathbed confessions happen so frequently because, in the light of our imminent demise and disappearance, preserving the old fearful identity that kept the secret is seen to be absurd, almost laughable; we are suddenly not the thing we have been defending all along. In the shadow of our disappearance we come to understand that the preservation of our name and our identity have taken enormous effort and willpower to sustain for a mere temporary and provisional sense of personhood. In leaving the stasis of secrecy we must commit to a new fidelity, and fluidity – a river flow of arrival – and not just on a temporary basis while the revelation is new, but shaped around a different life that calls for a deeper discipline: even if it is one we are just beginning to learn on our deathbed.

Confession, therefore, is not passive; is not the simple ability to face up to past wrongs; an active dynamic is foundational to the original meaning. In the early Christian tradition, *confession* meant the avowal and declaration of one's religion, to confess was to discover what one believed to be true by speaking it out loud before witnesses – often unsympathetic; to confess was to enter an axis of vulnerability and visibility, and sometimes to place oneself at the mercy of those who did not fully understand us in our struggle.

Declaring a new dispensation by confession, we see our trespasses against others in a new light, initiated by something we were hiding, not only from the world but from ourselves. Holding the secret was not only a defence against punishment but also a holding back from a next courageous step. To separate the confusion of punishment with revelation we first of all confess to ourselves, step onto solid ground in the privacy and spaciousness of our own hearts and minds, and then translate it into the best speech we have to represent it in the world, and by doing so attempt to meld two previously irreconcilable worlds. To confess is to integrate the offending with the offended, inside and out.

To confess is not only to acknowledge a truth we have held from ourselves all along, breathing quietly, alone and in secret what we could not initially give a voice, but a hopeful dedication to a larger power that might make us powerless to commit the self-same sin again.

COURAGE

is a word that tempts us to think outwardly, to run bravely against opposing fire, to do something under besieging circumstance, and perhaps, above all, to be seen to do it in public, to show courage: to be celebrated in story, rewarded with medals, given the accolade. But a look at its linguistic origins is to look in a more interior direction, and toward its original template, the old Norman French *coeur*, or heart.

Courage is the measure of our heartfelt participation with life, with another, with a community, a work; a future. To be courageous is not necessarily to go anywhere or do anything, except to make conscious those things we already feel deeply and then to live through the unending vulnerabilities of those consequences. To be courageous is to seat our feelings deeply in the body and in the world: to live up to and into the necessities of relationships that often already exist, with things we find we already care deeply about: with a person, a future, a possibility in society, or with an unknown that begs us on – and always has begged us on. To be courageous is to stay close to the way we are made.

The French philosopher Camus used to tell himself quietly to *live to the point of tears*, not as a call for maudlin sentimentality, but as an invitation to the deep privilege of belonging, and the way belonging affects us, shapes us and breaks our heart at a fundamental level. It is a fundamental dynamic of human incarnation to be moved by what we feel, as if surprised by the actuality and privilege of love and affection and its possible loss. Courage is what love looks like when tested by the simple everyday necessities of being alive.

From the inside, it can feel like confusion; only slowly do we learn what we really care about, and allow our outer life to be realigned in that gravitational pull. With maturity, that robust vulnerability comes to feel like the only necessary way forward, the only real invitation, and the surest, safest ground from which to step. On the inside we come to know who and what and how we love and what we can do to deepen that love; only from the outside, and only by looking back, does it look like courage.

CRISIS

is unavoidable. Every human life seems to be drawn eventually, as if by some unspoken parallel, some tidal flow or underground magnetic field, toward the raw, dynamic essentials of its existence, as if everything up to that point had been a preparation for a meeting, for a confrontation in an elemental form with our essential flaw, and with what an individual could, until then, only receive stepped down, interpreted or diluted.

This experience of absolute contact with an essential hidden dynamic, now understood to be essential to our lives, often ignored but now making itself felt, where the touchable rawness of life becomes part of the fabric of the everyday, and a robust luminous vulnerability becomes shot through with the necessary, imminent and inevitable prospect of loss, has been described for centuries as the dark night of the soul: *La noche oscura del alma.* But perhaps this dark night could be more accurately described as the meeting of two immense storm fronts, the squally vulnerable edge between what overwhelms human beings from the inside and what overpowers them from the outside.

The waveform that overwhelms a maturing human being from the inside is the inescapable nature of their own flaws and weaknesses, their self-deceptions and their attempts to create false names and stories to place themselves in the world; the felt need to control the narrative of the story around them with no regard to outside revelation. The immense wave on the outside is the invitation to give that self up, to be borne off by the wave and renamed, revealed and re-ordered by the powerful flow.

Walking the pilgrim edge between the two, holding them together, is the hardest place to stay, to breathe of both and make a world of both and to be active in their exchange: aware of our need to be needed, our wish to be seen, our constant need for help and succour, but inhabiting a world of luminosity and intensity, subject to the wind and the weather, surrounded by the music of existence, able to be found by the living world and with a wild, self-forgetful ability to respond to its call when needed; a rehearsal, in fact, for the act of dying, a place where inside and outside can reverse and flow with no fixed form.

DENIAL

is deeply underestimated as a state of being. Denial is an ever-present and even splendid thing when seen in the light of its merciful and elemental powers to cradle and hold an identity until it is ready to move on. Faced with the depth of loss and disappearance in the average life, a measure of denial is creative, necessary and self-compassionate: children are not meant to know they are one day to die and older adults are not meant to tell them. Refusing to face what we are not yet ripe and ready to face can help us to live through the more than enough difficulties of the present.

Denial fully experienced also enables us to understand the full measure of our reluctance to be here, thus becoming a pathway to self-knowledge, a way of both paying attention to and appreciating what is asking to be seen. Denial is a beautiful transitional state every human being inhabits before they are emancipated into the next, larger context and orphaned, often against their will, from their old and very familiar home.

Denial is ever present and unavoidable in a human life, even in the most accomplished guru, even in the Dalai Lama; it is a necessary dynamic, so that the overpowering elements of a waiting, terrifying universe can be held for now, over the horizon. Denial belongs to us all and should not be given away lightly.

Denial can be a prison if inhabited in too concrete and unmoving a way, but denial is also a necessary stepping-stone and a compassionate foundation for viewing those unable to take the next courageous step.

Denial can be a beautiful skin shed, left to be seen, or even to beautify, and beatify others as they follow, wearing our former clothes. To understand the true nature of our reluctance through observing and then inhabiting our denial is to see directly into the soul's wish to participate.

All of us live with temporary names and temporary stories, which allow us to breathe the air of the present while looking into the eyes of enormous powers that make up our immediate horizon of understanding. Denial comes to a natural end through the force of attention and intentionality to this horizon; much better to pay attention to what beckons than to try to look at what, by definition, we are not ready to look at.

To live in denial is to be in very good company. Denial is the crossroads between perception and readiness; to deny denial is to invite powers into our lives we have not yet readied ourselves to meet.

DESPAIR

takes us in when we have nowhere else to go: when we feel the heart cannot break any more, when our world or our loved ones disappear, when we feel we cannot be loved or do not deserve to be loved, when our God disappoints, or when our body is carrying profound pain in a way that does not seem to go away.

Despair is a haven with its own temporary form of strange beauty and self-compassion; it is the invitation we accept when we want to remove ourselves from hurt. Despair is a last protection. To disappear through despair is to seek a temporary but necessary illusion, a place where we hope nothing can ever find us in the same way again.

Despair is a necessary and seasonal state of repair, a temporary healing absence, an internal physiological and psychological winter when our previous forms of participation in the world take a rest; it is a loss of horizon; it is the place we go when we do not want to be found in the same way any more. We give up hope when certain particular wishes are no longer able to come true and despair is the time in which we both endure and heal, even when we have not yet found the new form of hope.

Despair is, surprisingly, the last bastion of hope; the wish being that if we cannot be found in the old way we cannot ever be touched or hurt in that same way again. Despair is the sweet but illusory abstraction of leaving the body while still inhabiting it, so we can stop the body from feeling any more. Despair is the place we go when we no longer want to make a home in the world and where we feel, with a beautifully cruel form of satisfaction, that we may never have deserved that home in the first place. Despair, strangely, has its own sense of achievement, and despair, even more strangely, needs despair to keep it alive.

Despair turns to depression and abstraction when we try to make it stay beyond its appointed season and start to shape our identity around its frozen disappointments. But despair can only stay beyond its appointed time through the forced artificiality of created distance, by abstracting ourselves from bodily feeling, by trapping ourselves in the disappointed mind, by convincing ourselves that the seasons have stopped and can never turn again, and perhaps, most simply and importantly, by refusing to let the body breathe by itself, fully and deeply. Despair is kept alive by freezing our sense of time and the rhythms of time; when we no longer feel imprisoned by time, and when the season is allowed to turn, despair cannot survive.

To keep despair alive we have to abstract and immobilise our bodies, our faculties of hearing, touch and smell, and keep the surrounding springtime of the world at a distance. Despair needs a certain tending, a reinforcing, and isolation, but the body left to itself will breathe, the ears will hear the first birdsong of morning or catch the leaves being touched by the wind in the trees, and the wind will blow away even the greyest cloud, will move even the most immovable season; the heart will continue to beat and the world, we realise, will never stop or go away.

The antidote to despair is not to be found in the brave attempt to cheer ourselves up with happy abstracts, but in paying a profound and courageous attention to the body and the breath, independent of our imprisoning thoughts and stories, even, surprisingly, in paying attention to despair itself, and the way we hold on to it, and which we realise was never ours to own and to hold in the first place. To see and experience despair fully in our body is to begin to see it as a necessary, seasonal visitation, and the first step in letting it have its own life, neither holding it nor moving it on before its time.

We take the first steps out of despair by taking on its full weight and coming fully to ground in our wish not to be here. We let our bodies and we let our world breathe again. In that breathing, despair cannot do anything but change into something else, into some other season, as it was meant to do from the beginning. Despair is a difficult, beautiful necessary, a binding understanding between human beings caught in a fierce and difficult world where half of our experience is mediated by loss, but it is a season, a waveform passing through the body, not a prison surrounding us. A season left to itself will always move, however slowly, under its own patience, power and volition.

Refusing to despair about despair itself, we can let despair have its own natural life and take a first step onto the foundational ground of human compassion, the ability to see and understand and touch, and even speak, the heartfelt grief of another.

DESTINY

always has a possessor, as in my destiny or your destiny or her destiny; it gives a sense of something we cannot avoid or something waiting for us; it is a word of storybook or mythic dimension. Destiny is hardly used in everyday conversation; it is a word that invites belief or disbelief: we reject the ordering of events by some fated, unseen force or we agree that there seems to be a greater hand than our own, working at the edges of even the most average life. But speaking of destiny not only grants us a sense of our own possibilities but gives us an intimation of our flaws: we sense, along with Shakespeare, that what is unresolved or unspoken in human character might overwhelm the better part of ourselves.

When we choose between these two poles, of mythic triumph or fated failure, we may miss the everyday conversational essence of destiny: our future influenced by the very way we hold the conversation of life itself, never mind any actions we might take or neglect to take. Two people, simply by looking at the future in radically different ways, have completely different futures awaiting them, no matter their immediate course of action. Even the same course of action, coming from a different way of shaping the conversation, will result in a different outcome. We are shaped by our shaping of the world and are shaped again in turn. The way we face the world alters the face we see in the world.

Strangely, every person always lives out their destiny, no matter what they do, according to the way they shape the conversation, but that destiny may be lived out on the level of consummation or complete frustration, through experiencing a homecoming or a distant sense of exile, or more likely some gradation along the spectrum that lies between. It is still our destiny, our life, but the sense of satisfaction involved and the possibility of fulfilling its promise may depend upon a brave participation, a willingness to hazard ourselves in a difficult world, a certain form of wild generosity with our gifts; a familiarity with our own depth, our own discovered, surprising breadth; and always, a long practised and robust vulnerability equal to what any future may offer. Our destiny is fated not only by great powers beyond our beckoning horizon but by the very way we shape and hold the everyday conversations of a familiar life.

DISAPPOINTMENT

is inescapable but necessary; a misunderstood mercy and, when approached properly, an agency for transformation and the hidden, underground engine of trust and generosity in a human life. The attempt to create a life devoid of disappointment is the attempt to avoid the vulnerabilities that make the conversations of life real, moving, and life-like; it is the attempt to avoid our own necessary and merciful heartbreak. To be disappointed is to reassess our self and our inner world, and to be called to the larger foundational reality that lies beyond any false self we had only projected upon the outer world.

What we call disappointment may be just the first stage of our emancipation into the next greater pattern of existence. To be disappointed is to reappraise not only reality itself but our foundational relationship to the pattern of events, places and people that surround us, and which, until we were properly disappointed, we had misinterpreted and misunderstood; disappointment is the first, fruitful foundation of genuine heartbreak from which we risk ourselves in a marriage, in a work, in a friendship, or with life itself.

The measure of our courage is the measure of our willingness to embrace disappointment, to turn towards it rather than away; the understanding that every real conversation of life involves having our hearts broken somewhere along the way and that there is no sincere path we can follow where we will not be fully and immeasurably let down and brought to earth, where what initially looks like a betrayal eventually puts real ground under our feet.

The great question in disappointment is whether we allow it to bring us to ground, to a firmer sense of our self, a surer sense of our world, and what is good and possible for us in that world, or whether we experience it only as a wound that makes us retreat from further participation.

Disappointment is a friend to transformation, a call

to both accuracy and generosity in the assessment of our self and others, a test of sincerity and a catalyst of resilience. Disappointment is just the initial meeting with the frontier of an evolving life, an invitation to reality, which we expected to be one particular way and turns out to be another, often something more difficult, more overwhelming and strangely, in the end, more rewarding.

FORGIVENESS

is a heartache and difficult to achieve because, strangely, it not only refuses to eliminate the original wound but actually draws us closer to its source. To approach forgiveness is to close in on the nature of the hurt itself, the only remedy being, as we approach its raw centre, to reimagine our relation to it.

It may be that the part of us that was struck and hurt can never forgive, that, remarkably, forgiveness never arises from the part of us that was actually wounded. The wounded self may be the part of us incapable of forgetting, and perhaps not actually meant to forget, as if, like the foundational dynamics of the physiological immune system, our psychological defences must remember and organise against any future attacks – after all, the identity of the one who must forgive is actually founded on the very fact of having been wounded.

Stranger still, it is that wounded, branded, un-forgetting part of us that eventually makes forgiveness an act of compassion rather than one of simple forget-ting. To forgive is to assume a larger identity than the person who was first hurt, to mature and bring to fruition an identity that can put its arm not only around the afflicted one within but also around the memories seared within us by the original blow, and through a kind of psychological virtuosity extend our understanding to one who first delivered it.

Forgiveness is a skill, a way of preserving clarity, sanity and generosity in an individual life, a beautiful question and a way of shaping the mind to a future we want for ourselves; an admittance that if forgiveness comes through understanding, and if understanding is just a matter of time and application then we might as well begin forgiving right at the beginning of any drama rather than put ourselves through the full cycle of festering, incapacitation, reluctant healing and even-tual blessing.

To forgive is to put oneself in a larger gravitational

field of experience than the one that first seemed to hurt us. We reimagine ourselves in the light of our maturity and we reimagine the past in the light of our new identity; we allow ourselves to be gifted by a story larger than the story that first hurt us and left us bereft.

The great mercy is that the sincere act of trying to forgive, even if it is not entirely successful, is a form of blessing and forgiveness itself.

At the end of life, the wish to be forgiven is ultimately the chief desire of almost every human being. In refusing to wait, in extending forgiveness to others now, we begin the long journey of becoming the person who will be large enough, able enough and generous enough to receive, at the very end, that absolution ourselves.

FRIENDSHIP

is a mirror to presence and a testament to forgiveness. Friendship not only helps us see ourselves through another's eyes, but can be sustained over the years only with someone who has repeatedly forgiven us for our trespasses, as we must find it in ourselves to forgive them in turn.

A friend knows our difficulties and shadows, and remains in sight, a companion to our vulnerabilities more than our triumphs, when we are under the strange illusion we do not need them. An undercurrent of real friendship is a blessing exactly because its elemental form is rediscovered again and again through understanding and mercy. All friendships of any length are based on a continued, mutual forgiveness. Without tolerance and mercy all friendships die.

In the course of the years, a close friendship will always reveal the shadow in the other as much as ourselves; to remain friends we must know the other and their difficulties, and even their sins, and encourage the best in them, not through critique but through addressing the better part of them, the leading creative edge of their incarnation, thus subtly discouraging what makes them smaller, less generous, less of themselves.

Through the eyes of a real friendship an individual is larger than their everyday actions, and through the eyes of another we receive a greater sense of our own personhood, one we can aspire to, the one in whom they have most faith. Friendship is a moving frontier of understanding, not only of the self and the other but also of a possible and as yet unlived future.

Friendship is the great hidden transmuter of all relationships: it can transform a troubled marriage, make honourable a professional rivalry, make sense of heartbreak and unrequited love, and become the newly discovered ground for a mature parent–child relationship.

The dynamic of friendship is almost always under-estimated as a constant force in human life. A

diminishing circle of friends is the first terrible diagnostic of a life in deep trouble: of overwork, of too
much emphasis on a professional identity, of forgetting
who will be there when our armoured personalities
run into the inevitable natural disasters and vulnerabilities found in even the most average existence.

Through the eyes of a friend we especially learn to
remain at least a little interesting to others. When we
flatten our personalities and lose our curiosity in the
life of the world or of another, friendship loses spirit
and animation. Boredom is the second great killer of
friendship.

Through the natural surprises of a relationship held
through the passage of years we recognise the greater
surprising circles of which we are a part and the faithfulness that leads to a wider sense of revelation,
independent of *human* relationship: to learn to be
friends with the earth and the sky, with the horizon
and with the seasons, even with the disappearances of
winter, and in that faithfulness take the difficult path
of becoming a good friend to our own going.

Friendship transcends disappearance: an enduring friendship goes on after death, the exchange only transmuted by absence, the relationship advancing and maturing in a silent internal conversational way, even after one half of the bond has passed on.

But no matter the medicinal virtues of being a true friend or sustaining a long, close relationship with another, the ultimate touchstone of friendship is not improvement, neither of the other nor of the self: the ultimate touchstone is *witness*, the privilege of having been *seen* by someone and the equal privilege of being granted the sight of the essence of another, to have walked with them and to have believed in them, and sometimes just to have accompanied them for however brief a span, on a journey impossible to accomplish alone.

GENIUS

is, by its original definition, something we already possess. Genius is best understood in its foundational and ancient sense, describing the specific underlying quality of a given place, as in the Latin *genius loci*, the spirit of a place; it describes a form of meeting, of air and land and trees, perhaps a hillside, a cliff edge, a flowing stream or a bridge across a river. It is the conversation of elements that makes a place incarnate, fully itself. It is the breeze on our skin, the particular freshness and odours of the water, or of the mountain or the sky in a given, actual geographical realm. You could go to many other places in the world with a cliff edge, a stream, a bridge, but it would not have the particular spirit or characteristic, the ambiance or the climate of this particular meeting place.

By virtue of its latitudes and longitudes, its prevailing winds, the aroma and colour of its vegetation, and the way a certain angle of the sun catches it in the cool early morning, it is a unique confluence, existing nowhere else on earth. If the genius of place is the meeting place of all the elements that make it up, then, in the same way, human genius lies in the geography of the body and its conversation with the world.

The human body constitutes a live geography, as does the spirit and the identity that abides within it. To live one's genius might be to dwell easily at the crossing point where all the elements of our life and our inheritance join and make a meeting. We might think of ourselves as each like a created geography, a confluence of inherited flows. Each one of us has a unique signature, inherited from our ancestors, our landscape, our language, and alongside it a half-hidden geology of our life as it has been lived: memories, hurts, triumphs and stories that have not yet been fully told. Each one of us is also a changing seasonal weather front, and what blows through us is made up not only of the gifts and heartbreaks of our own growing but also of our ancestors and the stories consciously and unconsciously passed to us about their lives.

To live out our genius is to live out the conversation between our particular inherited body and the body of the world from which we seem to have been made. Genius might not be a fixed platform where we can arrive solely through accomplishment; it is more likely the ability to live and breathe at the place where our particular, individual physical body meets all the other bodies of the world, corporeal and elemental: a body breathed over by wind, shaken by interior tremors, and washed away and rearranged by periodic floods; it has its own hard-won language and its attempts to order the un-orderable, but it also must follow the seasons, its own forms of happiness, and its particular and necessary griefs. It intuits a particular future for itself but is made in conversation with all other futures.

Genius is both a specific gift and a possibility that has not yet occurred; it is not a fixed internal commodity to be exploited and brought to the surface, but a conversation to be followed, deepened, understood and celebrated. Genius is the meeting between inheritance and horizon, between what has been told, what can be told and what is yet to be told, between our practical abilities and our relationship to the gravitational mystery that pulls us on. Our genius is to understand, and stand beneath the set of stars present at our birth, and from that place to seek the hidden, single star, over the night horizon, we did not know we were following.

GIVING

is a difficult and almost contemplative art form that can only be done well through practice; to learn to give is almost always the simple, sometimes heartbreaking act of just giving again. To stop giving in any relational situation is to call an end to that particular form of togetherness. Giving may be an essence of existence, and a test of our character; it asks deep questions about our relationship to others, to ourselves and, strangely, to time itself: all gifts change with the maturation of their recipients.

To give well, appropriately and often is to establish a beautiful seasonal symmetry between the urgency within us that wishes to be generous, and the part of the world that is suddenly surprised and happy to receive. To give generously but appropriately, and then – most difficult of all, and as the full apotheosis of the art – with feeling, in the moment and spontaneously has always been recognised as one of the greatest of human qualities.

Giving is not done easily; giving is difficult. Giving well is, in fact, a discipline that must be practised and observed over years to be done properly. The apprenticeship to the art often involves giving the wrong thing to the wrong person at the wrong time, and learning how to do the opposite through time and trial; it means getting beyond the boundaries of our own needs; it means understanding another and another's life. Most importantly, it acknowledges implicitly that we ourselves must be recipients of things we cannot often identify or even find ourselves.

Giving has an enormous horizon and a breadth that is hard to compass: it is both a practicality – it creates bonds and dependencies necessary to our communal well-being – and an essentiality – the essence of giving being that the other person is simply alive and, by corollary, not only a privilege to know but a living privilege themselves, who has the astonishing ability to acknowledge both the somebody who has given and the something that is given to them. As far as we know, no other corner of creation but a human being has the ability to fully acknowledge the spirit of another in this way.

Giving means paying attention and creating imaginative contact with the one to whom we are giving; it is a form of attention itself, a way of acknowledging and giving thanks for lives other than our own.

The first step in giving may be to create a budget, to make a list or to browse a shopfront or the web, but the essential deed is done through the door of contemplation: of the person, the charity, the cause, finding the essence of the need, the person or the relationship. Out of this image comes the surprise of understanding and the ability again to surprise the recipient by showing that someone else understands them and, through a display of virtuosity, can even identify needs they cannot admit themselves. The full genius of gift-giving is found when we give what a person does not fully feel they deserve, but that does not overstretch the point; it is the appropriate but surprising next step in their lives. It disarms and moves and empowers all at once, while gratifying the one who gives beyond most everyday satisfactions.

To give is to make an imaginative journey and put oneself in the body, the mind and the anticipation of another. To give is to make our own identities more real in the world by committing to something specific in the other person and something tangible that could represent that quality. To give is also to carry out the difficult task of putting something of our own essence in what we have given. The perfect gift may be tiny and inexpensive, but accompanied by a note that moves the recipient; the perfect gift may be enormous, extravagant, expensive and jaw-dropping as a courageous act of flamboyance and devil-may-care love, but to give appropriately always involves a tiny act of courage, a step of coming to meet, of saying I see you, and appreciate you and am also making an implicit promise for the future. Little wonder, then, that the holiday giving that is none of these – that is automatic, chore-based, 'walking round the shopping centre'-based – exhausts us, debilitates us, and in the end is quite often subtly insulting to the one to whom we eventually give the random item.

Better to spend a long time sitting in our armchairs in silent contemplation of those we want to gift, looking for the imaginative doorway that says I know you and see you and this is how I give thanks for you, which may bring us to the perfect *objet* but also may bring us instead to write the short heartfelt message that acknowledges their place in our lives. (*Nota bene*, rarely appropriate with children!)

Clichés are clichés, often because they are so stubbornly true: it is the thought that counts, but even more, it is the imagination behind the thought that counts, made tangible through gifts that find their definition through being twice blessed.

GRATITUDE

is not a passive response to something we have been given; gratitude arises from paying attention, from being awake in the presence of everything that lives within and without us. Gratitude is not necessarily something that is shown after the event; it is the deep, a priori state of attention that shows we understand and are equal to the gifted nature of life.

Gratitude is the understanding that many millions of things come together and live together and mesh together and breathe together in order for us to take even one more breath of air, that the underlying gift of life and incarnation as a living, participating human being is a privilege, that we are miraculously part of something, rather than nothing. Even if that something is temporarily pain or despair, we inhabit a living world, with real faces, real voices, laughter, the colour blue, the green of the fields, the freshness

of a cold wind, or the tawny hue of a winter landscape.

To see the full, miraculous essentiality of the colour
blue is to be grateful with no necessity for a word
of thanks. To see fully the beauty of a daughter's face
is to be fully grateful without having to seek a
God to thank him. To sit among friends and
strangers, hearing many voices, strange opinions; to
intuit inner lives beneath surface lives, to inhabit
many worlds at once in this world, to be a
someone amongst all other someones, and therefore
to make a conversation without saying a word, is
to deepen our sense of presence and therefore
our natural sense of thankfulness that everything
happens both with us and without us, that we
are participant and witness all at once.

Thankfulness finds its full measure in generosity of
presence, both through participation and witness. We
sit at the table as part of every other person's world
while making our own world without will or effort;
this is what is extraordinary and gifted, this is the

essence of gratefulness, seeing to the heart of privilege. Thanksgiving happens when our sense of presence meets all other presences. Being unappreciative might mean we are simply not paying attention.

GROUND

is what lies beneath our feet. It is the place where we already stand; a state of recognition, the place or the circumstances to which we belong, whether we wish to or not. It is what holds and supports us, but also what we do not want to be true: it is what challenges us, physically or psychologically, irrespective of our hoped for needs. It is the living, underlying foundation that tells us what we are, where we are, what season we are in and what, no matter what we wish in the abstract, is about to happen in our body, in the world or in the conversation between the two.

To come to ground is to find a home in circumstances, and in the very physical body we inhabit in the midst of those circumstances, and above all to face the truth, no matter how difficult that truth may be; to come to ground is to begin the courageous conversation, to step into difficulty, and, by taking that first step, begin the movement through all difficulties, to find the support and foundation that has been beneath our feet all along: a place to step onto, a place on which to stand, and a place from which to step.

HAUNTED

is a word that denotes an unresolved parallel, a presence that is not quite a presence; a visitation by the as yet unspeakable. It is also emblematic of the longing for incarnation, of an unbearable substrate of wanting, of not finding a home in this world or in the next, someone or something that walks the halls of our house or our mind looking for what will help to lay its own self to rest.

What haunts us is always something that seeks its own disappearance: it wants to become fully itself and so depart. If we feel continually haunted, over time we begin to become ghost-like ourselves and roam with intent whilst not quite knowing the object of our intention. Looking in the mirror, our face begins to look like our not-quite-incarnated life. We walk not exactly existing in the world we visit. Like the spirits and half-beings we imitate at Halloween, we roam the streets as if looking for an abode on this earth we are unable to locate, demanding tribute from those who dwell within. The exorcism of an unwanted spirit is consistent the world over: an invitation to return home; for it and for us to find our way back, to cease our restless ways and to quit disturbing others' lives or walking their houses by night.

We cease to be haunted when we cease to be afraid of making what has been untouchable real and touchable again: especially our understandings of the past, and especially those we wronged, those we were wronged by, or those we did not help. We become real by forgiving ourselves, and we forgive ourselves most authentically by changing the foundational pattern of our behaviour, especially our behaviour to those we have hurt. A fear of ghosts, or a fear of our own haunted mind, is the measure of our absence in this world. We cease to be afraid when we give away what was never ours in the first place and begin to be present to our own lives just as we find them, in our earthly vulnerabilities, even in facing what we have banished from our thoughts and made homeless, even when we do not know the way forward ourselves. When we make a friend of what we previously could not face, what once haunted us now becomes an invisible, parallel ally, a beckoning hand to our future.

We banish the misaligned when we align with what we are called to; we become visible and real when we give our gift and stop waiting for the gift to be given to us. We wake into our lives again, as if for the first time, laying to rest what previously had no home, through beginning to speak, beginning to make real and beginning to live, those elements constellating inside us that long to move from the invisible to the visible.

HEARTBREAK

is unpreventable: the natural outcome of caring for people and things over which we have no control, of holding in our affections those who inevitably move beyond our line of sight. Even the longest marriage has had its heart broken many times just in the many acts of staying together.

Heartbreak begins the moment we are asked to let go but cannot. In other words, it colours and inhabits and magnifies each and every day. Heartbreak is not a visitation, but a path that human beings follow through even the most average life. Heartbreak is an indication of our sincerity: in a love relationship, in a life's work, in trying to learn a musical instrument, in the attempt to shape a better, more generous self. Heartbreak is the beautifully helpless side of love and affection, and is just as much an essence and emblem of care as the spiritual athlete's quick but abstract ability to let go. Heartbreak has its own way of inhabiting time, and its own beautiful and trying patience in coming and going.

Heartbreak is how we mature. Yet we use the word 'heartbreak' as if it only occurs when things have gone wrong: an unrequited love, a shattered dream, a child lost before their time. Heartbreak, we hope, is something we can avoid; something to guard against, a chasm to be carefully looked for and then walked around. The hope is to find a way to place our feet where the elemental forces of life will keep us in the manner to which we want to be accustomed and which will keep us from the losses that all other human beings have experienced, without exception, since the beginning of conscious time. But heartbreak may be the very essence of being human, of being on the journey from here to there, and of coming to care deeply for what we find along the way.

Our hope to circumvent heartbreak in adulthood is beautifully and ironically childlike: heartbreak is as inescapable and inevitable as breathing, a part and a parcel of every path, asking for its due in every sincere course an individual takes. It may be that there may be not only *no* real life without the raw revelation of heartbreak but *no single path* we can take within a life that will allow us to escape without having that imaginative organ we call the heart broken by what it holds and then has to let go.

In a sobering physical sense, every heart does eventually break, as the precipitating reason for death or because the rest of the body has given up before it and it can no longer sustain its steady beat. But hearts also break in an imaginative and psychological sense: there is almost no path a human being can follow that does not lead to heartbreak. A marriage, a committed vow to another, even in the most settled, loving relationship, will always break our hearts at one time or another; as mentioned, a successful marriage has often had its heart broken many times just in order for the couple to stay together; parenthood, no matter the sincerity of our love for a child, will always break the mould of our motherly or fatherly hopes; a good work, seriously taken, will often take everything we have and still leave us wanting; and finally, even the most self-compassionate self-examination should, if we are sincere, lead eventually to existential disappointment.

Realising its inescapable nature, we can see heartbreak not as the end of the road or the cessation of hope but as the close embrace of the essence of what we have wanted or are about to lose. It is the hidden DNA of our relationship with life, outlining outer forms even when we do not feel it by the intimate physical experience generated by its absence; it can also ground us truly in whatever grief we are experiencing, set us to planting a seed with what we have left, or appreciate what we have built even as we stand in its ruins.

If heartbreak is inevitable and inescapable, it might be asking us to look for it and make friends with it, to see it as our constant and instructive companion, and even perhaps in the depth of its impact, as well as in its hindsight, to see it as its own reward. Heartbreak asks us not to look for an alternative path, because there is no alternative path. It is an introduction to what we love and have loved, an inescapable and often beautiful question, something or someone that has been with us all along, asking us to be ready to let go of the way we are holding things, and preparation perhaps for the last letting go of all.

HELP

is strangely something we want to do without, as if
the very idea disturbs and blurs the boundaries of our
individual endeavours, as if we cannot face how much
we need in order to go on. We are born with an
absolute necessity for help, grow well only with a
continuous succession of extended hands, and as adults
depend upon others for our further successes and
possibilities in life even as competent individuals. Even
the most solitary writer needs a reader, the most
Machiavellian mobster a trusted lieutenant, the most
independent candidate a voter.

Not only does the need for help never leave us
alone, but we must apprentice ourselves to its different,
necessary forms at each particular threshold of our
lives. At every stage we are dependent on our ability
to ask for specific forms of help at very specific times
and in very specific ways. Even at the end, the dignity

of our going depends on others' willingness to help us die well, the sincerity of their help often commensurate to the help we extended to them in our own life. Every transformation has at its heart the need to ask for the right kind of generosity.

An impending birth certainly means we look for aid: a place for it to occur, midwives, a doctor, a husband or partner to be present, a nest in which to welcome the child, a job to support a new life. And the one who is born needs endless help, food from the breast, walking and carrying at night, changes, washes, clothes, and a great deal of cooing and clucking.

The parents of those who need help need another kind of help themselves: their very own parents, parents of other children, playmates for the child, sometimes copious amounts of red wine and neverending amounts of sleep. They also need a new perspective, a new imagination for the next stage of their relationship. Romance is temporarily in abeyance, logistics loom over all; hands are full, but the relationship itself needs a helping hand.

But whether we are parents or not, there are two kinds of generosity and help for which we must continually ask, at every stage in our existence: visible help and invisible help. Visible help is most often practical or transactional help: we pay for a bed or a meal, or we pay someone to work for us. But it may be that it is the second, less easily recognisable and invisible help which is most crucial for stepping into the unknown. Though we can think of invisible help in the old sense of an intervention from angelic or parallel worlds, we can also think of it in an everyday, practical way: invisible help is the help we as yet do not know we need. Invisible help is the help we are always not quite ready for; all we can do is shape our identity toward being surprised, toward paying attention to what is just about to appear over the horizon of our understanding.

This overwhelming need for help never really changes in a human life from the first day we are brought from the womb calling lustily for that commodity. We need extraordinary physical help to get through our first years, continued help through our childhood, and extraordinary emotional help and good luck to get through our adolescence. After that, the need for continual help becomes more subtle, hidden as it is by the illusion that we are suddenly free agents able to survive on our own, the one corner of the universe able to supply its own answers.

It may be that the ability to know the necessity for help, to know how to look for that help, and then, most importantly, how to ask for it, is one of the primary transformative dynamics that allows us to emancipate ourselves into each new epoch of our lives. Without the understanding that we need a particular form of aid at every crucial threshold in our lives, and without the robust vulnerability in asking for that help, we cannot pass through the door that bars us from the next dispensation of our lives: we cannot birth ourselves.

To ask for visible and invisible help, and to ask for the right kind of help and to feel that it is no less than our due – that, in effect, we deserve both a visible and an invisible helping hand – may be an engine of transformation itself. The need for help, our greatest vulnerability, may be the very door through which we must pass in order to open the next horizon of our lives.

In the end comes also our beginning, the ancient sense of a door opening to some final unknown, some invisible voice attempting to help us come to terms with our own disappearance, the hand extended to help us over a horizon equally as mysterious as the one we crossed at our birth.

HIDING

is a way of staying alive. Hiding is a way of holding ourselves until we are ready to come into the light. Hiding is one of the brilliant and virtuoso practices of almost every part of the natural world: the protective quiet of an icy northern landscape, the held bud of a future summer rose, the snowbound internal pulse of the hibernating bear. Hiding is underestimated. We are hidden by life in our mother's womb until we grow and ready ourselves for our first appearance in the lighted world; to appear too early in that world is to find ourselves with the immediate necessity for outside intensive care.

Hiding done properly is the internal faithful promise for a proper future emergence, as embryos, as children or even as emerging adults in retreat from the names that have caught us and imprisoned us, often in ways where we have been too easily seen and too easily named.

We live in a time of the dissected soul, the immediate disclosure: our thoughts, imaginings and longings
exposed to the light too much, too early and too often;
our best qualities squeezed too soon into a world
already awash with ideas that oppress our sense of self
and our sense of others. What is real is almost always,
to begin with, hidden, and does not want to be understood by the part of our mind that mistakenly thinks
it knows what is happening. What is precious inside
us does not care to be known by the mind in ways
that diminish its presence.

Hiding is an act of freedom from the misunderstanding of others, especially in the enclosing world
of oppressive secret government and private entities,
attempting to name us, to anticipate us, to leave us
with no place to hide and grow in ways unmanaged
by a creeping necessity for absolute naming, absolute
tracking and absolute control. Hiding is a bid for
independence – from others, from mistaken ideas we
have about ourselves, from an oppressive and mistaken
wish to keep us completely safe, completely ministered

to, and therefore completely managed. Hiding is creative, necessary and beautifully subversive of outside interference and control. Hiding leaves life to itself, to become more of itself. Hiding is the radical independence necessary for our emergence into the light of a proper human future.

HONESTY

is reached through the doorway of grief and loss. Where we cannot go in our mind, our memory or our body is where we cannot be straight with another, with the world, or with our self. The fear of loss, in one form or another, is the motivator behind all conscious and unconscious dishonesties: all of us are afraid of loss, in all its forms; all of us, at times, are haunted or overwhelmed by the possibility of a disappearance; and all of us, therefore, are one short step away from dishonesty. Every human being dwells intimately close to a door of revelation they are afraid to pass through. Honesty lies in understanding our close and necessary relationship with not wanting to hear the truth.

The ability to speak the truth is as much the ability to describe what it is like to stand in trepidation at this door as it is to actually go through it and become that beautifully honest spiritual warrior, equal to all circumstances, we would like to become. Honesty is not the revealing of some foundational truth that gives us power over life or another, or even the self, but a robust incarnation into the unknown unfolding vulnerability of existence, where we acknowledge how powerless we feel, how little we actually know, how afraid we are of not knowing, and how astonished we are by the generous measure of loss that is conferred upon even the most average life.

Honesty is grounded in humility, and indeed in humiliation, and in admitting exactly where we are powerless. Honesty is not found in revealing the truth, but in understanding how deeply afraid of it we are. To become honest is, in effect, to become fully and robustly incarnated into powerlessness. Honesty allows us to live with not knowing. We do not know the full story, we do not know where we are in the story; we do not know who is at fault or who will carry the blame in the end. Honesty is not a weapon to keep loss and heartbreak at bay; honesty is the outer diagnostic of our ability to come to ground in reality, the hardest attainable ground of all, the place where we actually dwell. The living, breathing frontier, where there is no realistic choice between gain or loss.

ISTANBUL

lies in the Western imagination like a bridge, a crossing point, a meeting of history and cultures, a background to exoticism and novelistic adventure, but holds the simultaneous ability to be both a threshold and a closed door, a bridge to nowhere, a place where questions stop being asked as much as a place where they begin; a place difficult, in effect, for the visiting Western mind to travel on from.

All the more intense a place to stand, then, between one world ending and some unknown otherness on the other side, on the Galata Bridge, with the sun falling back into the extinguished West on one side and the moon rising flame yellow and darkened red over that place we have arbitrarily called the East. Between the known and the unknown, Istanbul lives and breathes like a real human being, the balustrades of the bridge crowded with balletic fishermen curving their long rods ritualistically back over their heads like a well-practised chorus, and then dropping their lines into the choppy, boat-ploughed waters of the Golden Horn. Istanbul knows from whence it comes in our imaginations, but knows not yet where it goes.

South and west of Istanbul lie the ruins of Troy, haloed for three thousand years by the Western mind, but further south down the coast stretch a ribbon of more contemporary holiday towns, places that now receive European invasions of a different kind. As the coast turns east and begins to brush north of Cyprus it moves out of the Western mind altogether. Few in the West know where Turkey joins Syria. Even less is known about the interior of the country. Turkey is a periphery to the Western mind; Istanbul a crowded bridge into a centre that, to the Western imagination, does not quite exist.

Its own periphery studded with new high-rise buildings, glinting and winking in the fading light from the west, the future seems to crowd from the edge as if besieging an older, even more ancient Istanbul; the heart of the city beats on in its labyrinthine streets and bazaars, piled high with spices and the shaded spectra of saffron, turmeric, and the rising stacks of brilliant cloth and wedged, red-gold, pure, sticky honeycomb.

Walking in the spice market of Istanbul after the antiseptic wrapping of the developed West, we are enveloped by a shouting, calling, hectoring, affectionate, begrudging, beseeching, begging, laughing humanity. Inhaling the scent and vision of the stalls, our atrophied senses begin to bud and bloom: the fresh fried fish doled out on flatbreads from the boats moored on the glinting dusky waters, the braided tunnels of shops leading to other tunnels of shops in the Grand Bazaar. The piles of pomegranates, the heaps of turmeric and the wafted scent of saffron from the stalls remind us we are never just one thing, never just one set of senses, that we are no one name: we are Constantinople and Istanbul, and even Stamboul, and we have carried this frontier between the past and the present with us all our lives, as this city has. We are an ecology within a hundred other ecologies, a noisy meeting place, a bridge from a directly perceived outer world leading to an indirect, unknown and as yet unspoken interior. We live now, but all our history, and even our future, is already occurring, even as we walk the street, fading into the jubilant evening light of a day, strangely, and even reluctantly, already beginning to end.

JOY

is a meeting place, of deep intentionality and of self-forgetting, the bodily alchemy of what lies inside us in communion with what formerly seemed outside, but is now neither, but become a living frontier, a voice speaking between us and the world: dance, laughter, affection, skin touching skin, singing in the car, music in the kitchen, the quiet irreplaceable and companionable presence of a daughter. The sheer intoxicating beauty of the world inhabited as an edge between what we previously thought was us and what we thought was radically other than us.

Joy may be made by hard-won, practised achievement as much as by an unlooked for, passing act of grace arrived out of nowhere; joy, to our consternation, is a measure of our relationship to death and our living with death; joy is the act of giving ourselves away before we need to or are asked to; joy is practised generosity.

If joy is a deep form of abiding love, it is also the raw engagement with the passing seasonality of exist-ence, the fleeting presence of those we love understood as gift; what is, and will never be again, going in and out of our lives: faces, voices, memory, aromas of the first spring day or a wood fire in winter, the last breath of a dying parent stored in the memory as they create a rare, raw, beautiful frontier between loving presence and blossoming absence.

To feel a full and untrammelled joy is to have become fully generous; to allow ourselves to be joyful is to have walked through the doorway of fear, the dropping away of the anxious, worried self, felt like a thankful death itself, a disappearance, a giving away, overheard in the laughter of friendship, the vulner-ability of happiness and the vulnerability of its imminent loss, felt suddenly as a strength, a solace and a source: the claiming of our place in the living conversation, the sheer privilege of being in the presence of a mountain, a sky or a well-loved familiar face. I was here, and you were here, and together we made a world.

LONELINESS

is the doorway to unspoken and yet unspecified desire. In the bodily pain of aloneness is the first step to understanding how far we are from a real friendship, from a proper work or a long-sought love. Loneliness can be a prison, a place from which we look out at a world we cannot inhabit; loneliness can be a bodily ache and a penance, but loneliness fully inhabited also becomes the voice that asks and calls for that great unknown someone or something we want to call our own.

Loneliness is the very state that births the courage to continue calling, and when fully lived can undergo its own beautiful reversal, becoming in its consummation the far horizon that answers back.

In the grand scale of things, loneliness is a privilege. Human beings may have the ability to feel aloneness as no other creature can, with a power magnified by intelligence and imagination. Animals may feel alone in an instinctual way, moving naturally and affectionately toward others of their kind, but human beings may be the only beings that can articulate, imagine or call for a specific life they feel they might be missing.

Loneliness is the substrate and foundation of belonging, the gravitational field that draws us home, and in the beautiful essence of its isolation, the hand reaching out for togetherness. To allow ourselves to feel fully alone is to allow ourselves to understand the particular nature of our solitary incarnation; to make aloneness a friend is to apprentice ourselves to the foundation from which we make our invitation to others. To feel alone is to face the truth of our irremediable and unutterable singularity, but a singularity that can kiss, create a conversation, make a vow or forge a shared life. In the world or community, this essential singularity joins with others through vision, intellect and ideas to make a society.

Loneliness is not a concept, it is the body constellating, attempting to become proximate and even join with other bodies, through physical touch, through conversation or the mediation of the intellect and the imagination.

Loneliness is the place from which we pay real attention to voices other than our own; being alone allows us to find the healing power in the other. The shortest line in the briefest e-mail can heal, embolden, welcome home and enliven the most isolated identity. Lonely human beings are lonely because they are made to belong. Loneliness is a single malt taste of the very essentiality that makes conscious belonging possible. The doorway is closer than we think. I am alone; therefore, I belong.

LONGING

is the transfiguration of aloneness, the defenceless
interior secret core of a person receiving its overdue
invitation from the moon, the stars, the night horizon,
and the great tidal flows of life and love. Longing is
divine discontent; the unendurable present, finding a
physical doorway to awe and discovery that frightens
and emboldens, humiliates and beckons, makes us into
pilgrim souls and sets us on a road that starts in the
centre of the body and then leads out, like an uncaring
invitation, like a comet's tail, felt like both an unre-
lenting ache and a tidal pull at one and the same time,
making us willing to give up our perfect house, our
paid-for home and our accumulated belongings.

Longing is felt through the lens and ache of the
body, magnifying and bringing the horizon close, as if
the horizon were both a lifetime's journey away and
living deep inside at some unknown core – as if we

were coming home into a beautifully familiar, condensed strangeness.

In the longing and possession of romantic love, it is as if the body has been loaned to someone else but has then, from some remote place, taken over the senses – we no longer know ourselves.

Longing calls for a beautiful, grounded humiliation, the abasement of what we thought we were, and strangely the giving up of central control while being granted a new, watchful, scintillating, peripheral discrimination. The static, wilful central identity is pierced and wounded, violated and orphaned into its own future, as if set adrift on a tide: like Moses in his floating cradle, bumping along the reeds of the Nile; like a child lost in a panicked, moving crowd; and, at times, like a creature stunned, gripped and lifted by a passing hawk.

Longing has its own secret, future destination, and its own seasonal emergence from within, a ripening from the core, a seed growing in our own bodies; it is as if we are put into a relationship with an enormous distance inside us, leading back to some unknown origin with its own secret timing, indifferent to our wills, and gifted at the same time with an intimate sense of proximity, to a lover, to a future, to a transformation, to a life we want for ourselves, and to the beauty of the sky and the ground that surrounds us.

Longing is nothing without its dangerous edge, which cuts and wounds us while setting us free, and beckons us exactly because of the human need to invite the right kind of peril. The foundational instinct that we are here essentially to risk ourselves in the world, that we are a form of invitation to others and to otherness, that we are meant to hazard ourselves for the right thing, for the right woman or the right man, for a son or a daughter, for the right work, or for a gift given against all the odds. In longing we move, and are moving, from a known but abstracted elsewhere to a beautiful, about-to-be-reached someone, something, or somewhere we want to call our own.

MATURITY

is the ability to live fully and equally in multiple
contexts, most especially the ability, despite our many
griefs and losses, to courageously inhabit the past, the
present and the future all at once. The wisdom that
comes from maturity is recognised through a disci-
plined refusal to choose between or isolate three
powerful dynamics that form human identity: what
has happened, what only looks as if it is happening
now, and what is about to occur.

Immaturity is shown by making false choices: living
only in the past, or only in the present, or only in
the future, or even living only two out of the three.

Maturity is not a static arrived platform, a golden
epoch from where life is viewed from a calm,
untouched oasis of wisdom, but the dissolution of
living elemental frontiers between what has happened,
what is happening now, and the consequences of our

past; first imagined anew, and then lived into the waiting future.

Maturity is the breakdown of elemental frontiers, between different epochs of our life, between life and death, between the part of us that has been a fine, upstanding citizen and the darker, helpless parts of us that have caused harm and damage. Maturity is the time when these tidal forces meet and break apart our life, making one life out of our regrets, our self-compassion, and our forgiveness forged into a future made real by a radical change in our behaviour: real maturity can only be sustained by real silence, by a daily discipline of silence and an inhabitation of spaciousness, a foundational giving away. Maturity is the discipline of giving up and giving away, to see what is left and what is real.

Maturity calls us to risk ourselves as much as we did in our immaturity, but for a bigger picture, a larger horizon; for a powerfully generous outward incarnation of our inward qualities and not for gains that make us smaller, even in the winning.

Our previous stage of immaturity always beckons, offering a false haven and false accounting, an ersatz safety in one state or the other: a hiding place and disappearance in the past, a false isolation of the present, or an unobtainable sure prediction of the future. But maturity beckons also, asking us to be larger, more fluid, more elemental, less cornered, less unilateral; a living, conversational intuition between the inherited story, the one we are privileged to inhabit, and the one – if we are large enough and broad enough, moveable enough and, even, here enough – just, astonishingly, about to occur.

MEMORY

is not just a then, recalled in a now; the past is never just the past: memory is a pulse passing through all created life, a waveform, a *then* continually becoming other *thens*, all the while creating a continual but almost untouchable now. But the present fashionable obsession with living only in the now misunderstands the multi-layered inheritance of existence, where all epochs live and breathe in parallels.

Whether it be the epochal moment initiated by the appearance of the first hydrogen atoms in the universe, or a first glimpse of adulthood perceived in adolescence, or the raw physical remembrance of holding our first child in our arms, memory passes through an individual human life like a building musical waveform, constantly maturing, increasingly virtuosic, often volatile, sometimes overpowering. Every human life holds the power of this immense inherited pulse, holds and then supercharges it, according to the way we inhabit our identities in the untouchable now. Memory is an invitation to the source of our life, to a fuller participation in the now, to a future about to happen, but ultimately to a frontier identity that holds them all at once. Memory makes the now fully inhabitable.

The genius of human memory is firstly its very creation through experience, and then the way it is laid down in the mind according to the identity we inhabited when we first decided to remember, then its outward radiating effect, and then all its possible future outcomes, occurring all at the same time and able to change alongside the person who is remembering. We actually inhabit memory as a living threshold, as a place of choice and volition and imagination, a crossroads where our future diverges according to how we interpret, or perhaps more accurately how we live, the story we have inherited. We can be overwhelmed, traumatised, made smaller by the tide that brought us here, we can even be drowned and disappeared by memory; or we can spin a cocoon of insulation to protect ourselves and bob along passively in the wake of what we think has occurred, but we also have other, more engaging possibilities; memory, in a sense, is the very essence of the conversation we hold as individual human beings. A full inhabitation of memory makes human beings conscious, a living connection between what has been, what is and what is about to be. Robbed of our memory by Alzheimer's or by a stroke, we lose our identities. Memory is the living link to personal freedom.

Through the gift of an inheritance truly inhabited, we come to understand that memory creates and influences what is about to happen, and has little to do with what we quaintly, and often unimaginatively, call the past. We might recall the ancient Greek world where Memory was always understood to be the mother of the muses, meaning that all of her nine imaginative daughters, all of the nine forms of human creative endeavour recognised by the ancient Greek

imagination, and longed for by individuals and societies to this day, were born from the womb and the
body of memory.

NAMING

love too early is a beautiful but harrowing human difficulty. Most of our heartbreak comes from attempting to name who or what we love, and the way we love, too early in the vulnerable journey of discovery.

We can never know in the beginning, in giving ourselves to a person, to a work, to a marriage or to a cause, exactly what kind of love we are involved with. When we demand a certain, specific kind of reciprocation before the revelation has flowered completely, we find ourselves disappointed and bereaved, and in that grief may miss the particular form of love that is actually possible but that did not meet our initial and too specific expectations. Feeling bereft, we take our identity as one who is disappointed in love, our almost proud disappointment preventing us from seeing the lack of reciprocation from the person or the situation as simply a difficult invitation into a deeper and as yet unrecognisable form of affection.

The act of loving itself always becomes a path of humble apprenticeship, not only in following its difficult way and discovering its different forms of humility and beautiful abasement, but, strangely, through its fierce introduction to all its many astonishing and different forms, where we are asked continually and against our will to give in so many different ways, without knowing exactly, or in what way, when or how, the mysterious gift will be returned.

We name mostly in order to control, but what is worth loving does not want to be held within the bounds of too narrow a calling. In many ways love has already named us before we can even begin to speak back to it, before we can utter the right words or understand what has happened to us, or is continuing to happen to us: an invitation to the most difficult art of all, to love without naming at all.

NOSTALGIA

is the arriving waveform of a dynamic past, newly remembered and about to be re-imagined by a mind and a body at last ready to come to terms with what actually occurred. Nostalgia subverts the present by its overwhelming physical connection to a person or a place – to a time in which we lived or to a person with whom we lived – making us wonder, in the meeting of past and present, if the intervening years ever occurred. Nostalgia can feel like an indulgence, a sickness, an inundation by forces beyond us, but, strangely, forces that have also lived with us and within us all along.

Nostalgia is not indulgence. Nostalgia tells us we are in the presence of imminent revelation, about to break through the present structures held together by the way we have remembered: something we thought we understood but that we are now about to fully understand; something already lived but not fully lived, issuing not from our future but from something already experienced; something that was important, but something to which we did not grant importance enough; something now wanting to be lived again, at the depth to which it first invited us but which we originally refused.

Nostalgia is not an immersion in the past; nostalgia is the first annunciation that the past as we know it is coming to an end.

PAIN

is the doorway to the here and now. Physical or emotional pain is an ultimate form of ground, saying, to each of us, in effect, there is no other place than this place, no other body than this body, no other limb or joint or pang or sharpness or heartbreak but this searing presence, refusing to go away. Pain asks us to heal by focusing not only on the place the pain is felt but also the actual way the pain is felt. Pain is a form of alertness and particularity; pain is a way in.

Through the radical undoing and debilitation of repeated pain we are reacquainted with the essentialities of place and time and existence itself; in deep pain we have energy only for what we can do wholeheartedly, and then only within a narrow range of motion, metaphorically or physically, from tying our shoelace to holding the essential core conversations that are reciprocal and reinforcing within the closed-in circle of those we love. Pain teaches us a fine economy, in movement, in the heart's affections, in what we ask of ourselves, and eventually in what we ask in others.

Pain's beautiful humiliations make us naturally humble and force us to put aside the guise of pretence. In real pain we have no other choice but to learn to ask for help, and on a daily basis. Pain tells us we belong and cannot live forever alone or in isolation. Pain makes us understand reciprocation. In real pain we often have nothing to give back other than our own gratitude, a smile that perhaps looks half like a grimace or the passing friendship of the thankful moment to a helpful stranger, and pain can be an introduction to real friendship, it tests those friends we think we already have, but also introduces us to those who newly and surprisingly come to our aid.

Pain is the first proper step to real compassion; it can be a foundation for understanding all those who struggle with their existence. Experiencing real pain ourselves, our moral superiority comes to an end; we stop urging others to get with the programme, to get their act together or to sharpen up, and start to look for the particular form of debilitation, visible or invisible, that every person struggles to overcome. In pain, we suddenly find our understanding and compassion engaged as to why others may find it hard to fully participate.

Strangely, the narrow focus that is the central, difficult invitation of bodily pain calls for a greater perspective, for a bigger, more generous sense of humour. With the grand perspective, real pain is never far from real laughter – at ourselves, or for another watching that self; laughter at the predicament or the physical absurdity that has become a daily experience. Pain makes drama of an everyday life: with our body and our presence firmly caught on stage and in the spotlight, we are visible to others in a way over which we have no choice, bending this way or that, limping here or leaning there.

Lastly, pain is appreciation for, most of all, the simple possibility and gift of a pain-free life – all the rest is a miraculous bonus. Others do not know the gift in simply being healthy, of being unconsciously free to move or walk or run. Pain is a lonely road, no one can know the measure of our particular agonies, but through pain we have the possibility, just the possibility, of coming to know others as we have, with so much difficulty, and through so much suffering, come to know ourselves.

PARALLELS

are not what we think. Parallels do not really exist except in a mathematical sense and except as an idea to play off. If it is difficult for anything in the real world to move in a true straight line, think of the impossibility of two things moving together in two parallel straight lines. In the human imagination a parallel world is not a world that replicates the one in which we live, or is its exact opposite, but one that turns and flows through many other possibilities and dimensionalities, all the while keeping company and somehow referencing the one it shadows. The parallel life is as unpredictable and indeterminate as the one that supposedly gave it its life.

When we speak of parallels, we speak therefore of accompanying possibilities, like a life or a partner we did not choose, the refusal of an uncertain other life influencing this certain and familiar present life. We evolve as much with the parallel as we do with the present; as the years pass, our relationship to the path not taken or the person we did not pursue changes as much as it does with the one we did. There are many deathbeds where the path not taken is far more real and present than the one actually chosen; the man or the woman abandoned far more real than the wife or husband dutifully lived with for years.

There is also the question of depth: we may have taken a certain path, but only half-heartedly, without conviction, sacrifice, bravery or sincerity. The under-lying depth below our surface approach waits for us like an invitation and a reproach, an ocean seen from a cliff: another life, informing this life. On the one hand, a spur to boldness and a deeper participation when we realise how much in this life the other life breathes, or on the other, if distanced into the abstract, a source of shame, a life un-braved, un-lived, misun-derstood, no matter how much it whispered conspiratorially in our ears. A parallel life we never fully invited into our own.

PILGRIM

is a word and a name that every human being might
be given, at least temporarily, as an accurate assessment
of their essence: a stranger to be waved at in passing,
or met along the way; a someone always passing
through very quickly; a someone on their way to
somewhere else, never quite knowing whether the
destination or the path stands first in importance;
someone who underneath it all doesn't quite understand from whence they came or quite where they
are going, and many times from where their next bite
of bread will come; someone dependent on help from
other strangers and from those who will meet them
along the way.

Travelling toward a place over the horizon, a pilgrim
is almost by definition someone abroad in a world of
impending revelation, where something is always about
to happen or be revealed, including, most fearfully, and

as part of their eventual arrival, a strange rehearsal for their own disappearance.

The great measure of the pilgrim journey of human maturation is the increasing understanding that we move through life in the blink of an eye; that we are not long with the privilege of having eyes to see, ears to hear, a voice with which to speak and arms to put round a loved one; that we are simply passing through. We are creatures made real through contact, meeting and then moving on; creatures who, saying hello and saying goodbye, strangely, never get to choose one above the other. Human life is a contact; a getting to know, and then a moving beyond which is never ceasing, from the transformations that enlarge and strengthen us to the ones that turn us from consuming to being consumed, from seeing to being semi-blind, from speaking in one voice to hearing in another.

The defining experience at the diamond-hard centre of reality is eternal movement as beautiful and fearful invitation: a beckoning dynamic, asking us to move from this to that. The courageous pilgrim life is the life that is equal to this unceasing tidal and seasonal becoming: and surprisingly, beneath it all, stillness, a friendship with silence being the only proper physical preparation for joining the breathing autonomic exchange of existence. We are so much made of movement that we speak intuitively of the destination being both inside us and beyond us; we sense we are the journey along the way, the one who makes it and the one who has already arrived. We are still running around the house packing our bags and we have already gone and come back, even in our preparations; we are alone in the journey and we are just about to meet the people we have known for years.

But if we are all movement, exchange and getting to know, where a refusal to move on makes us unreal, we are also journeymen and journeywomen, with an unstoppable need to bring our skills and experience, our voice and our presence to good use in the eternal now we visit along the way. We want to belong and be useful as we travel. We are creatures of movement, but we have something immutable in the flow: an elemental, essential nature that gives a person a name and a voice and a character as they flow on. We take our first bubbling source and our broad, subsequent confluences and grow in the conversation between them, all the way to our dissolution in the sea.

We give ourselves to that final destination as an ultimate initiation into vulnerability and arrival, not ever truly knowing what lies on the other side of the transition, or if we survive it in any recognisable form. Strangely, our arrival at that last transition along the way is exactly where we have the opportunity to understand who might have made the journey and to appreciate the privilege of having existed as a particularity, an immutable person; a trajectory whole and of itself.

In that perspective it might be that faith, reliability, responsibility and being true to something unspeakable are possible even if we are travellers, and that we are made better, more faithful companions, indeed *pilgrims*, on the astonishing, never-to-be-repeated journey by combining the precious memory of the *then* with the astonishing but taken for granted experience of the *now*, and both with the unbelievable, and hardly possible, *just about to happen.*

PROCRASTINATION

is not what it seems. What looks from the outside like our delay, our lack of commitment, even our laziness, may have more to do with a slow, necessary ripening through time, and the central struggle with the realities of any endeavour to which we have set our minds. To hate our procrastinating tendencies is in some way to hate our relationship with time itself, to be unequal to the phenomenology of revelation and the way it works its own way, in its very own gifted time, only emerging when the very qualities it represents have a firm correspondence in our necessarily struggling heart and imagination.

Procrastination when studied closely can be a beautiful thing, a parallel with patience, a companionable friend; a revealer of the true pattern already, we are surprised to find, caught within us: acknowledging, for instance, as a writer, that before a book can be written, most of the ways it cannot be written must be tried first, in our minds – on the blank screen, on the empty page, or staring at the bedroom ceiling at four in the morning. Procrastination enables us to taste the single malt essence of our own reluctance.

An endeavour achieved without delay, wrong turnings, occasional blank walls and a vein of self-doubt running through all, leading eventually to some degree of heartbreak, is a thing of the moment, a bagatelle, and often neither use nor ornament. It will be scanned for a moment and put aside. What is worthwhile carries the struggle of the maker written within it, but wrought into the shape of an earned understanding.

Procrastination helps us to be a student of our own reluctance, to understand the hidden darker side of the first enthusiastic idea, to learn what we are afraid of in the endeavour itself; to put an underbelly into the work itself so that it becomes a living, satisfying whole, not a surface trying to manipulate us in the moment.

Procrastination does not stop a project from coming to fruition; what stops us is giving up on an original idea because we have not got to the heart of the reason we are delaying, nor let the true form of our reluctance instruct us in the way ahead. To procrastinate is to be involved with larger entities than our own ideas, to refuse to settle for an early underachieving outcome and wrestle like Jacob with his angel, finding, as Rilke said, 'Winning does not tempt that man. This is how he grows, by being defeated, decisively, by greater and greater beings.'

REGRET

is a short, evocative and achingly beautiful word; an elegy to lost possibilities, even in its brief annunciation, it is also a rarity and almost never heard except where the speaker insists that they have none, that they are brave and forward-looking and could not possibly imagine their life in any other way than the way it is. To admit regret is to understand we are fallible, that there are powers in the world beyond us; to admit regret is to lose control not only of a difficult past but of the very story we tell about our present. And yet, strangely, to admit sincere and abiding regret is one of our greatest but unspoken contemporary sins.

The rarity of honest regret may be due to our contemporary emphasis on the youthful perspective – it may be that a true, useful regret is not a possibility or a province of youth, that it takes a hard-won maturity to experience the depths of regret in ways that do not overwhelm and debilitate us but put us into a proper, more generous relationship with the future. Except for brief senses of having missed a tide, having hurt another, having taken what is not ours, youth is not yet ready for the rich current of abiding regret that runs through and emboldens a mature human life.

Sincere regret may, in fact, be a faculty for paying attention to the future, for sensing a new tide where we missed a previous one, for experiencing timelessness with a grandchild where we neglected a boy of our own. To regret fully is to appreciate how high the stakes are in even the average human life.

Fully experienced, regret turns our eyes, attentive and alert, to a future possibly lived better than our past.

REST

is the conversation between what we love to do and how we love to be. Rest is the essence of giving and receiving; an act of remembering, imaginatively and intellectually, but also psychologically and physically. To rest is to give up on the already exhausted will as the prime motivator of endeavour, with its endless outward need to reward itself through established goals. To rest is to give up on worrying and fretting, and the sense that there is something wrong with the world unless we are there to put it right; to rest is to fall back, literally or figuratively, from outer targets and shift the goal not to an inner, static bull's eye, an imagined state of perfect stillness, but to an inner state of natural exchange.

The template of rest is the natural exchange of the body breathing, the autonomic giving and receiving that forms the basis and the measure of life itself. We are rested when we are a living exchange between what lies inside and what lies outside, when we are an intriguing conversation between the potential that lies in our imagination and the possibilities for making that internal image real in the world; we are rested when we let things alone and let ourselves alone, to do what we do best, breathe as the body intended us to breathe, to walk as we were meant to walk, to live with the rhythm of a house and a home, giving and taking through cooking and cleaning. When we give and take in an easy, foundational way, we are closest to the authentic self, and closest to that authentic self when we are most rested. To rest is not self-indulgent; to rest is to prepare to give the best of ourselves, and to perhaps, most importantly, arrive at a place where we are able to understand what we have already been given.

In the first state of rest is the sense of stopping, of giving up on what we have been doing or how we have been being. In the second is the sense of slowly coming home, the physical journey into the body's uncoerced and unbullied self, as if trying to remember the way or even the destination itself. In the third state is a sense of healing and self-forgiveness and of arrival. In the fourth state, deep in the primal exchange of the breath, is the give and the take, the blessing and the being blessed, and the ability to delight in both. The fifth stage is a sense of absolute readiness and presence, a delight in and an anticipation of the world and all its forms; a sense of being the meeting itself between inner and outer, and that receiving and responding occur in one spontaneous movement.

A deep experience of rest is the template of perfection in the human imagination, a perspective from which we are able to perceive the outer specific forms of our work and our relationships whilst being nourished by the shared foundational gift of the breath itself. From this perspective we can be rested while putting together an elaborate meal for an arriving crowd, whilst climbing the highest mountain or sitting at home surrounded by the chaos of a loving family.

Rested, we are ready for the world but not held

hostage by it; rested, we care again for the right things and the right people in the right way. In rest we re-establish the goals that make us more generous, more courageous, more of an invitation, someone we want to remember, and someone others would want to remember too.

ROBUSTNESS

is a word denoting health, psychological or physical;
the ability to meet the world with vigour and impact.
To be robust is to be physically or imaginatively
present in the very firm presence of an equally robust
something or someone else. Being robust means we
acknowledge the living current in something other
than ourselves. Robustness is a measure of the live
frontier in a conversation, whether it is a physical
contact in a wrestling match, a good exchange of
ideas in the classroom or a marital argument in the
kitchen. Without robustness all relationships become
defined by their fragility, wither and begin to die.
To be robust is to attempt something and risk something beyond the perimeter of our own constituted
identity: to get beyond our own thoughts or the
edge of our own selfishness. Robustness and vulnerability belong together. To be robust is to show a

willingness to take collateral damage, to put up with temporary pain, noise, chaos, or our systems being temporarily undone. Robustness means we can veer off either side of the line while keeping a firm ongoing intent. Robustness is the essence of parenting: both of children and ideas.

A robust response always entertains the possibility of humiliation; it is also a kind of faith, a sense that we will somehow survive the impact of a vigorous meeting, though not perhaps in the manner to which we are accustomed.

A lack of robustness denotes ill-health, psychological or physical; it can feed on itself. The less contact we have with anything other than our own body, our own rhythm or the way we have arranged our life, the more afraid we can become of the frontier where actual noise, meetings and changes occur. To come out and meet the world again is to heal from isolation, from grief, from illness, from the powers and traumas that first robbed us of that meeting and of a vital sense of presence in the world; to be robust again is to leave the excuses we have made not to risk ourselves and to find ourselves alive once more in the encounter.

Robustness, almost as a contradiction, demands we find a calm centre in the midst of tumult. The quiet is what enables us to be cheerful in noise, equitable in the face of injustice, or calm in the face of attack. We also find in this quiet centre the deeper foundations of physical presence, the wide field that allows a wide, multicontextual conversational view of reality, where our experience approximates that of a large, loving, chaotic, happy family, full of cheerful argument, scrapes, high spirits and slammed doors, all sustained with the need for times of peace and quiet before we rejoin the fray. When our physical presence does fray, another form of internal presence must be found, another robustness to take us through. Robustness is not an option in most human lives, to choose its opposite is to become invisible.

ROME

is eternal only in the sense that disappearance is eternal. The sun-roasted city on an August afternoon, a living testament to the way nothing lasts in the form it is first constructed or understood. In the shaded, shimmering light that is the first invitation to evening, the ruins of the Forum or the Coliseum stand as silhouettes, one behind the other, whilst on the horizon behind the dome of St Peter's is lit by the last gold of a sun that sets on a city that forever lives in the last light of what has gone before. In Rome the present is accessible only through what is about to disappear.

Rome is a series of interpretations of the past, attempted by each fleeting present. In the city of splendour, pomp, power and empire, the spiritual materialism of the Vatican or the Coliseum find their temporary specifics, have their moment, and then are gone or will be gone. Here, human ideas and human endeavour find their fullest form only as a beautiful ruin.

Standing on the hot stone streets, the statue of Caesar Augustus stands against the sky, the marble hand beckoning to a future which will never come to pass and never could come to pass. The city of the eternal is actually the city that most celebrates the insubstantiality of human striving. What is imagined now, or what is dreamt of now, will never happen exactly as we wish, and things find their full beauty only in the wear and tear of weather, the patina of oxidation, and the actuality of human appearance and disappearance; what is abiding in human life is the actual daily conversation that occurs in the very shadow of the monuments we raise to our abstract desires.

Looking down over the darkening, thankfully un-eternal city, the discourse about our present and our possible future is made strangely beautiful by the privilege of walking amidst the decay and disappearance of so many past futures, as if we are being forgiven already for our too-specific hopes, when the general beautifying hand of time puts everything into such a multi-layered and satisfyingly unspecific perspective. Everything saying, sotto voce, that though we have our moment in the sun, we might be best understood, might even be most ourselves, as a beautiful ruin; most real when we are on our way out, or even gone altogether.

Only in maturity do we begin to understand that whatever citadel of thought or identity we have built and proudly displayed to others, whatever monuments to our achievements we attempt to leave behind, none of us know the true perspective with which we will be viewed or the way in which our memory will be enjoyed. Whether we finally manage to get to Italy or no, whether we walk the evening streets of the imperial city or not, all of us will surely, if we live long enough to gain the perspective, see Rome before we die.

RUN AWAY

is what most human beings would like to do a great
deal of the time. It is the *flight* part of the *fight or flight*
in our bodies and our past; it is our protection, an
evolutionary momentum and a biological memory
deep in the human body that allowed our ancestors
to survive to another day and bequeath to us, gener-
ations later, this day.

To want to run away is an essence of being human;
it transforms any staying through the transfigurations
of choice. To think about fleeing from circumstances,
from a marriage, a relationship or from a work is part
of the conversation itself and helps us understand the
true distilled nature of our own reluctance, thus
allowing us a deeper honesty about the cross-currents
of our difficulty in being fully present.

Strangely, we are perhaps most fully incarnated as
humans when part of us does not want to be here,

or doesn't know how to be here. Presence may be only fully understood and realised through fully understanding our reluctance to show up. To understand the part of us that wants nothing to do with the full necessities of work, of relationships, of doing what is required, is to learn humility, to cultivate self-compassion, and to sharpen that sense of humour essential to a merciful perspective of both a self and another.

Wanting to run is necessary; actual running can save our lives at crucial times, but it can also be extremely dangerous and unwise, especially in the presence of animals that are bigger, faster and more agile than we are, especially when the very act of running triggers an aggressive predatory response, or when running exiles us from the very circumstances that were about to mature and cultivate our character. In the wild, the best response to dangerous circumstances is often not to run but to assume a profoundly attentive identity, to pay attention to what seems to threaten and, in that attention, not to assume the identity of the victim.

Through being equal to fierce circumstances we make ourselves larger than the part of us that wants to flee, while not losing its protective understandings about when it might be appropriate. Besides, there is rarely one discrete identity who needs to run. We have many different constituencies inside and out. We are not only protectors of a multilayered self but also of our family and community, of children, of those who are infirm or temporarily incapacitated, or who simply have the wrong perspective. We decide not to run not only because there are many who would be left behind who cannot run as fast as we can, but also because, in turning to the source of the fear, we have the possibility of finding a different way forward, a larger good, through circumstances, rather than away from them in some supposedly safe area where threats no longer occur.

We know intuitively that most of the time we should not run, we should stay and look for a different way forward, despite the evolutionary necessity. Rarely is it good to run, though the rare times do sometimes prove the exception, but we are wiser, more present, more mature, more understanding when we realise we can never flee from the inner need to run away.

SELF-KNOWLEDGE

is not fully possible. We do not reside in a body, a mind or a world where it is achievable or, from the point of being interesting, even desirable. Half of what lies in the heart and mind is potentiality, resides in the darkness of the unspoken and unarticulated and has not yet come into being; this hidden, unspoken half of a person will supplant and subvert any present understandings we have about ourselves.

Human beings are always, and always will be, a frontier between what is known and what is not known. The act of turning any part of the unknown into the known is simply an invitation for an equal measure of the unknown to flow in and re-establish that frontier: to reassert the far inward, as yet unknown horizon of an individual life; to make us what we are – that is, a moving edge between what we know about ourselves and what we are about to become. What we are actually about to become, or are afraid of becoming, always trumps and rules over what we *think* we are already.

The hope that a human being can achieve complete honesty and self-knowledge with regard to themselves is a fiction and a chimera, the jargon and goals of a corporate educational system brought to bear on the depths of an identity where the writ of organising language does not run.

Self-knowledge includes the understanding that the self we want to know is about to disappear. What we can understand is the way we occupy this frontier between the known and the unknown, the way we hold the conversation of life, the figure we cut at that edge, but a detailed audit of the self is not possible and diminishes us in the attempt to establish it. We are made on a grander scale, half afraid of ourselves, half in love with immensities beyond any name we can give.

Self-knowledge is often confused with transparency, but knowledge of the self always becomes the under-standing of the self as a confluence between what is know and not known; a flowing meeting of elements, including all the other innumerable selves in the world, not a set commodity to be unearthed, measured and knocked into shape. Self-knowledge is not clarity or transparency or knowing how everything works; self-knowledge is a fiercely attentive kind of frontier conversation with the unknown, a form of humility and thankfulness, a sense of the privilege of a particular form of participation, coming to know the way we hold the conversation of life and perhaps, above all, the miracle that there is a particular something rather than an abstracted nothing, and we are a very particular part of that particular something.

What we recognise and applaud as honesty and transparency in an individual is actually the humble demeanour of the apprentice, someone paying extreme attention – to themselves, to others, to life, to the next step, which they may survive or they may not; someone who does not have all the answers but who is attempting to learn what they can, about themselves and those with whom they share the journey; someone like everyone else, wondering what they and their society are about to turn into. We are neither what we think we are nor entirely what we are about to become, we are neither purely individual nor fully a creature of our community, but an act of becoming that can never be held in place by a false form of nomenclature. No matter our need to find a place to stand amidst the onward flow of the world, the real foundation of the self is not in self-knowledge, but in the self-forgetfulness that occurs when it meets something other than the self it first wanted to know.

SHADOW

does not exist by itself: it is cast, by a real, physical body. We may say a person is overwhelmed by their shadow – a Harvey Weinstein by their sexuality, a Richard Nixon by their overweening sense of power, a nation by its hubris – but their shadow is passive, an absence of light, a shape lent by their own outline. Shadow is shaped by presence; presence comes a priori to our flaws and absences. To change the shape of ourselves is to change the shape of the shadow we cast. To become transparent is to lose one's shadow altogether, something we often desire in the spiritual abstract but actually something that is not attainable by human beings – to change the shape of the identity that casts a shadow is more possible. Shadow is a necessary consequence of being in a sunlit, visible world, but it is not a central identity, or a power waiting to overwhelm us.

Even the most beneficial presence casts a shadow. Mythologically, having no shadow means being of another world, not being fully human, not being in or of this world. Shadow is something that must be lived with, literally, as it follows us around, obscuring the sun or the view for others, yet we cannot use it as an excuse not to be present, nor to act, nor to affect others by our presence, no matter if the effect is sometimes, indeed, overshadowing and difficult. Nor can we use it as an excuse to run uncaring over other's concerns.

To live with our shadow is to understand how human beings live at a frontier between light and dark, and to approach the central difficulty: that there is no possibility of a lighted perfection in this life; that the attempt to create it is often the attempt to be held unaccountable, to be the exception, to be the one who does not have to be present or participate, and therefore does not have to hurt or get hurt. To cast no shadow on others is to vacate the physical consequences of our appearance in the world.

Shadow is a beautiful, inverse confirmation of our incarnation. Shadow is intimated absence; almost a template of presence. It is a clue to the character of our appearance in the world. It is an intimation of the ultimate vulnerability, the dynamic of being found by others, not only through the physical body but by its passing acts; even our darkening effect on others; shadow makes a presence of absence, it is a clue to ourselves and to those we are with, even to the parts of ourselves not yet experienced, yet already perceived by others. Shadow is not good or bad, only inescapable.

SHYNESS

is the hallway of presence, the necessary doorway to new and deeper desires, the first necessary step in the maturation of an unexpected life, and arises from the sudden, often unwanted and difficult grounding that undergirds our experience of awe.

Shyness is the sense of a great unknown, suddenly about to be known, and suddenly become immensely personal, addressing us as if we might know what to say, where to put ourselves, or in the case of romance what to wear.

To feel shy is to look five ways at once: to the beckoning new life in front of us, to the line of retreat behind us, to alternative possibilities of escape to left and right, and in really difficult circumstances to look to the hope for a complete and sudden disappearance. Shyness is the first necessary crossroads on the path of becoming.

Shyness is underestimated and neglected as a way of being when first approaching the new, the necessary and the overwhelming. Without shyness, our over-confidence precludes us from the appropriate confusion, awkwardness and helplessness that accompanies the first stage of revelation. Without shyness we cannot shape an identity ripe for revelation.

Our visual media, especially television, tells us that shyness is unnecessary and thus corrupts our sense of what constitutes a real exploration. Likewise, in our virtual travels we rarely meet many beautiful representations of shyness through social media. But physical shyness tells us through our very vulnerability that we are at last in the presence of the mystery, of some thing, some place or someone we deeply desire or that represents what we desire, though we do not as yet, in our essential physical helplessness, know how to even begin the conversation to bring it about.

Shyness is the exquisite and vulnerable frontier between what we think is possible and what we think we deserve.

Without shyness it is not possible to apprehend the new. Total confidence at the beginning of a new phase of life means we are misinformed, that we are deeply mistaken, that we think we know what is about to occur and who we are about to become.

Shyness is an invitation to a particular form of beauty, to qualities that are meant to be both practised and cultivated; shyness is our friend; and the annunciation that we are just about to walk through the door and through all our difficulties, attempt another beginning.

SILENCE

is frightening. Silence is not stillness, but tidal and seasonal movement left to itself; an intimation of the end, the graveyard of fixed identities. Real silence puts any present understanding to shame, orphans us from certainty, leads us beyond the well-known and accepted reality, and confronts us with the unknown and previously unacceptable conversation about to break in upon our lives.

Silence does not end scepticism but makes it irrelevant. Belief or unbelief or any previously rehearsed story meets the wind in the trees, the distant horn in the busy harbour, or the watching eye and listening ear of a puzzled loved one.

In silence, essence speaks to us of essence itself and asks for a kind of unilateral disarmament, our own essential nature slowly emerging as the defended periphery atomises and falls apart. As the busy edge dissolves we begin to join the conversation through the portal of a present unknowing, robust vulnerability, revealing in the way we listen, a different ear, a more perceptive eye, an imagination refusing to come too early to a conclusion and belonging to a different person than the one who first entered the quiet.

Out of the quiet emerges the sheer incarnational presence of the world, a presence that seems to demand a moving, internal symmetry in the one breathing and listening equal to its own breathing, listening elemental powers.

To become deeply silent is not to become still, but to become tidal and seasonal, a coming and going that has its own inimitable, essential character, a story not fully told, like the background of the sea, or the rain falling, or the river going on, out of sight, out of our lives.

Reality met on its own terms demands absolute presence, and absolute giving away, an ability to live on equal terms with the fleeting and the eternal, the hardly touchable and the fully possible, a full bodily appearance and disappearance, a rested giving in and giving up; another identity braver, more generous and more here than the one looking hungrily for the easy, unearned answer.

SOLACE

is the art of asking the beautiful question, of ourselves, of our world, or of one another, in fiercely difficult and un-beautiful moments. Solace is what we must look for when the mind cannot bear the pain, the loss or the suffering that eventually touches every life and every endeavour; when longing does not come to fruition in a form we can recognise; when people we know and love disappear; when hope must take a different form than the one we have shaped for it.

Solace is the spacious, imaginative home we make where disappointment goes to be welcomed and reha-bilitated. When life does not in any way add up, we must turn to the part of us that has never wanted a life of simple calculation.

Solace is found in allowing the body's innate foundational wisdom to come to the fore, the part of us that already knows it is mortal and must take its leave like everything else, and leading us, when the mind cannot bear what it is seeing or hearing, to the bird-song in the tree above our heads, even as we are being told of a death, each note an essence of morning and of mourning, of the current of a life moving on, but somehow also, and most beautifully, carrying, bearing and even celebrating the life we have just lost – a life we could not see or appreciate until it was taken from us.

To be consoled is to be invited onto the terrible ground of beauty upon which our inevitable disap-pearance stands, to a voice that does not soothe falsely but touches the epicentre of our pain or articulates the essence of our loss, and then emancipates us into both life and death as an equal birthright.

Solace is not an evasion, nor a cure for our suffering, nor a made-up state of mind. Solace is a direct seeing and participation; a celebration of the beautiful coming and going, appearance and disappearance of which we have always been a part. Solace is not meant to be an answer but an invitation, through the door of pain and difficulty, to the depth of suffering and simultaneous beauty in the world that the strategic mind by itself cannot grasp nor make sense of.

To look for solace is to learn to ask fiercer and more exquisitely pointed questions, questions that reshape our identities and our bodies and our relation to others, even if they do not earn an answer. Standing in loss but not overwhelmed by it, we become useful and generous and compassionate and even more amusing companions for others. But solace also asks us very direct and forceful questions. Firstly, how will you bear the inevitable loss that will accompany you? And how will you endure its memory through the years? And above all, how will you shape a life equal to and as beautiful and as astonishing as a world that can birth you, bring you into the light, and then, just as you are beginning to understand it, take you away?

TOUCH

is what we desire in one form or another, even if we find it through being alone, through the agency of silence or through the felt need to walk at a distance: the meeting with something or someone other than ourselves, the light brush of grass on the skin, the ruffling breeze, the actual touch of another's hand; even the gentle first touch of an understanding which, until now, we were formerly afraid to hold.

Whether we touch only what we see, or the mystery of what lies beneath the veil of what we see, we are made for unending meeting and exchange, while having to hold a coherent mind and body, physically or imaginatively, which in turn can be found and touched itself. We are something for the world to run up against and rub up against: through the trials of love, through pain, through happiness, through our simple everyday movement through the world. And the world touches us in many ways, some of which are violations of the body or our hopes for safety: through natural disaster, through heartbreak, through illness, through death itself.

In the ancient world the touch of a god was seen as both a blessing and a violation at one and the same time. Being alive in the world means being found by that world and sometimes touched to the core in ways we would rather not experience. Growing with our bodies, all of us find ourselves at one time violated or wounded by this world in difficult ways, and still we live and breathe in this touchable, sensual world, and through trauma, through grief, through recovery, we heal in order to be touched again in the right way, as the physical consecration of a mutual, trusted invitation.

Nothing stops the body's arrival in each new present, except death itself, which is intuited in all cultures as another, ultimate, intimate form of meeting. Nothing stops our ageing nor our witness to time, asking us again and again to be present to each different present, to be touchable and findable, to be one who is living up to the very fierce consequences of being bodily present in the world.

To forge an untouchable, invulnerable identity is actually a sign of retreat from this world; of weakness; a sign of fear rather than strength, and betrays a strange misunderstanding of an abiding, foundational and necessary reality: that untouched, we disappear.

UNCONDITIONAL

love is not fully possible, unconditional love is the necessary dream-like destination where we never fully arrive. We are mortal creatures of living and dying, and how we love and what we love is conditional upon where we stand in the drama and the seasonality of our living and dying. Love may be sanctified and ennobled by its commitment to the unconditional horizon of perfection, but what makes love real in the human world seems to be our moving, struggling conversation with that wanted horizon rather than any possibility of arrival. The hope for, or the declaration of, a purely spiritual, unconditional love is more often a coded desire for immunity and safety, an attempt to forgo the trials of vulnerability, powerlessness and the exquisite pain to which we apprentice ourselves in a relationship, a marriage, in raising children, in a work we love and desire.

The hope for unconditional love is the hope for a different life than the one we have been given. Love is the conversation between possible, searing disappointment and a profoundly imagined sense of arrival and fulfilment: how we shape that conversation is the touchstone of our ability to love in the real, inhabited world. The true signature and perhaps even the miracle of human love is helplessness, and all the more miraculous because it is a helplessness which we wittingly or unwittingly choose: in our love of a child, a partner, a work or a road we have to take against the odds.

Our roads and journeys of love are always lived through beautiful humiliations, through disappointments and through forms of imprisonment: of our own or another's strange behaviour, or simply subject to the seasonality of the world – the arriving weather of existence always blowing through once-stable lives and, many times, blowing us apart.

Unconditional love is the beautiful, hoped-for impossibility, and yet we could not fully understand the nature of our helplessness without looking through the lens of that hoped-for perfection. We are creatures who do not get to choose between what we want and what is wanted of us, and we seem to embody the full vulnerabilities of love only when we dwell at the moving frontier between this wanting and being wanted. The invitation is made to us every day whether we desire it or no, to enter a deeply human world of robust vulnerability, shot through with a sometimes joyful, more often difficult, helplessness; to risk ourselves in the conditional world in which we live and to accept that there is no possible path we can follow where we will be untouched by the heartbreak, the difficulties and the joys that move us and move through us. The only path possible seems to be in giving our selves unconditionally to the conditionality of each overwhelming, disturbing and rewarding guise of love.

UNREQUITED

love is the love human beings experience most of the time. The very need to be fully requited may be to turn from the possibilities of love itself. Men and women have always had difficulty with the way a love returned hardly ever resembles a love given, but unrequited love may be the form that love mostly takes; for what affection is ever returned over time in the same measure or quality with which it is given? Every man or woman loves differently and uniquely, and each of us holds different dreams and hopes and falls in love or is the object of love at a very specific threshold in a very particular life where very, very particular qualities are needed for the next few years of our existence. What other human being could ever love us as we need to be loved? And whom could we know so well and so intimately through all the twists and turns of a given life that we could show them exactly the continuous and appropriate form of affection they need?

Requited love may happen, but it is a beautiful temporary, a seasonal blessing, the aligning of stars not too often in the same quarter of the heavens, an astonishing blessing. But it is a harvest coming only once every long cycle, and a burden to the mind and the imagination when we set that dynamic as the state to which we must always return in order to feel ourselves in a true, consistent, loving relationship.

Whether our affections are caught in romantic love, trying to see our neighbours as ourselves, or trying to love a great but distant God, our love rarely seems to be returned in the mode that it is given. That gift is returned in ways that, to begin with, we rarely recognise. Human beings live in disappointment and a self-appointed imprisonment when they refuse to love unless they are loved the selfsame way in return. It is the burden of marriage, the difficult invitation at the heart of parenting and the central difficulty in our relationship with any imagined, living future. The great discipline seems to be to give up wanting to control the manner in which we are requited, and to forgo the natural disappointment that flows from expecting an exact and measured reciprocation, from a partner, from a child, from our hopes for a loving God.

We seem to have been born into a world where love, except for brilliant, exceptional moments, seems to exist from one side only, ours, and that may be the difficulty and the revelation and the gift — to see love as the ultimate in giving and letting go — and through the doorway of that affection make the most difficult sacrifice of all, giving away the very thing we want to hold forever.

VULNERABILITY

is not a weakness, a passing indisposition, or something we can arrange to do without. Vulnerability is not a choice. Vulnerability is the underlying, ever-present and abiding undercurrent of our natural state. To run from vulnerability is to run from the essence of our nature; the attempt to be invulnerable is the vain attempt to become something we are not and, most especially, to close off our understanding of the grief of others. More seriously, in refusing our vulnerability we refuse the help needed at every turn of our existence and immobilise the essential, tidal and conversational foundations of our identity.

To have a temporary, isolated sense of power over all events and circumstances is a lovely, illusionary privilege, and perhaps the prime and most beautifully constructed conceit of being human – and especially of being youthfully human – but it is a privilege that must be surrendered with that same youth, with ill health, with accident, with the loss of loved ones who do not share our untouchable powers, powers eventually and most emphatically given up as we approach our last breath.

The only choice we have as we mature is how we inhabit our vulnerability, how we become larger and more courageous and more compassionate through our intimacy with disappearance; our choice is to inhabit vulnerability as generous citizens of loss, robustly and fully, or conversely as misers and complainers, reluctant and fearful, always at the gates of existence but never bravely and completely attempting to enter, never wanting to risk ourselves, never walking fully through the door.

WITHDRAWAL

can be the very best way of stepping forward, and done well – a beautiful, freeing act of mercy – and as an art form, underestimated in this time of constant action and engagement. So much of what we are involved with, in even the highest cause, becomes involvement at the busy periphery, where the central conversation has been lost to the outer edges of what was, to begin with, a very simple central invitation. Withdrawal is often not what it looks like – a disappearance – no, to withdraw from entanglement can be to appear again in the world in a very real way and begin the process of renewing the primary, essential invitation again.

Though life does seem determined to be a beautiful and entrancing distraction – just as we ourselves are a distraction to others, testing them as we test ourselves and our mutual sincerity – our participation in this dance of distraction also makes more real, and more necessary, our ability to return to essential ground, to an essential person or an essential work.

We stick to the wrong thing quite often, not because it will come to fruition by further effort but because we cannot let go of the way we have decided to tell the story, and we become further enmeshed even by trying to make sense of what entraps us, when what is needed is a simple, clean breaking away.

To remove ourselves entirely and absolutely, abruptly and at times uncompromisingly, is often the real and radically courageous break for freedom. Unsticking ourselves from the mythical Tar Baby, seemingly set up, just for us, right in the middle of our path, we start the process of losing our false enemies, and even our false friends, and most especially the false sense of self we have manufactured to live with them: we make ourselves available for the simple purification of seeing ourselves and our world more elementally and there-fore more clearly again. We withdraw, not to disappear but to find another ground from which to see; a solid ground from which to step, and from which to speak again, in a different way: a clear, rested, embodied voice, our life as a suddenly emphatic statement, one we can recognise as our own, and one from which, now, we have absolutely lost the wish to withdraw.